NORTHUMBRIAN
CROSSES OF THE PRE-NORMAN
AGE: by W. G. Collingwood M.A. F.S.A.

First published in 1927.
Reprinted in 1989 by Llanerch Enterprises,
Felinfach, Lampeter, Dyfed.
ISBN 0947992359

PREFACE

MANY books have been written about crosses. I own to having increased the output occasionally since 1899, when I completed my friend W. S. Calverley's posthumous papers on the early monuments of the diocese of Carlisle; and I am far from disparaging the industry and learning of any who have approached the tantalizing subject.

This book, however, has an aim of its own. It is an attempt to consider ancient styles as phases of a process, and to place the examples in series. Monographs on the more famous monuments are valuable; so are descriptive catalogues. They provide the material for classification. But until the classes are formed, and then connected into some reasonable scheme, we have not done all we can.

To do this convincingly a corpus of the whole body of known fragments would be required; but as there are roughly about a thousand separate pieces, such a work is not easy to handle in one volume. For details regarding stones not mentioned here I refer to articles contributed to the transactions of antiquarian societies, especially those of Yorkshire, Cumberland and Westmorland, Newcastle-upon-Tyne, Dumfriesshire and Galloway, and Derbyshire, whose officers I thank for leave to reproduce a number of illustrations.

Line-drawings rather than photographs are given because they show the facts of design disentangled from the accidents of wear and tear. The sketches are all by myself, and nearly all from direct study of the originals. I hope that what the text lacks the illustrations will supply; and that some readers finding pleasure, perhaps amusement, possibly surprise at the wealth of our pre-Norman art, will join in the desire to protect its remains from desecration.

Easter 1927.

W. G. C.

CONTENTS

NORTHUMBRIAN CROSSES

Chapter I. The Rude Stone Pillar

WHILE Britain was still under Roman government, tombstones were set up which seem to commemorate Christians. One such is built into Brougham Castle (Westmorland) evidently from the fort of Brovacum on the same site. It reads 'Tittus M[-] vixit annis plus minus xxxii. A[-] frater titulum [posuit]'; the form 'he lived thirty-two years *more or less*' is unlike the wording of pagan epitaphs, which are precise about the length of the subject's life. Hope of resurrection made the earthly course of the believer unimportant; and this alone is enough to distinguish a Christian monument in the fourth century. (R. G. Collingwood, Cumb. and Westmd. Ant. Soc. Trans. N.S. xxii, 141 f.)

A stone with lettering of that age (Fig. 1) was in 1891 found at Whithorn Priory Church. The Latin is barbarous; the meaning is definitely Christian, — 'We praise Thee, O Lord. Latinus, aged thirty-five years, and his daughter, aged four years. The descendants of Barrovados made the monument here.' If St Ninian's Candida Casa was founded at the close of the fourth century, this must be of its earliest period —a simple inscription without ornament and without even a separate cross to head the phrase, although the initial seems to be struck through with a bar, making it serve as a cross.

Near Trawsfynydd in Merioneth, N. Wales, is the Bedd (grave of) Porius. Its stone is similarly lettered in late Roman characters — 'Porius hic in tumulo iacit. Homo P¹IANVS fuit'; with a bar over the joined P¹, meaning the monogram for XPICTOC, Christ. And at Penmachno near Bettws-y-Coed is the inscription, also in late Roman letters, — 'Carausius hic iacit in hoc congeries [*sic*] lapidum', over which is the Chi-Rho or Chrismon, formed of + (for X) and P combined. This shape of the monogram occurs also in Cornwall on a stone at St Just-in-Penwith, inscribed 'Silus ic iacit'; but it is not the first form known in Britain, for Roman coins with XP combined were current, and the tin ingots from the Thames at Battersea (in the British Museum) bear the same symbol, and are apparently of the fourth century. The XP is seen again in Ceolfrid's dedication stone at Jarrow (A.D. 685); but as he was a scholar, perhaps he adopted the earlier form with antiquarian intent. On the whole the + P is the later, and its use in the stones we have next to consider suggests that they are by no means so early as the monument of Latinus.

Fig. 2 gives the rude pillar at Kirkmadrine in the Rhynns of Galloway inscribed 'A et (traces of Omega formerly visible). Hic iacent s[an]c[t]i et praecipui sacerdotes id es[t] Viventius et Mavorius', with the + P monogram. The form of the A, which is not one of the many Roman types of A but common from the seventh century onwards, suggests a date not before the later part of the sixth. 'The Kirkmadrine lettering is definitely later than that of the Paulinus and Vortipore stones (now at Carmarthen)

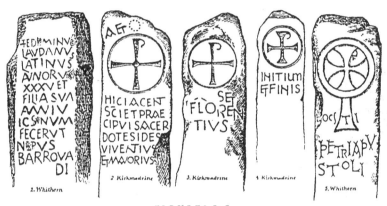

FIGURES 1-5

of the middle sixth century' (R. G. Collingwood, Trans. Dumfriesshire and Galloway Ant. Soc. 3rd ser. X, 210). Fig. 3 represents another stone to [—]s and Florentius at the same place, and Fig. 4 is a later example in which 'Initium et finis' means the same as the 'Alpha et Omega' of Fig. 2. It is later because the monogram is a coarsened form, and the joined minuscules 'um' and the shape of the N carry us away further from the Roman uncials of the first Christian period. We are now in the seventh century and these rude stones introduce us to the oldest of the Northumbrian crosses.

Some time after 660, when King Oswiu conquered the south of what is now Scotland, Anglian settlers began to inhabit Galloway. Before Bede finished his Ecclesiastical History (A.D. 731) there were so many of them that they had needed a bishop of their own race, and Pecthelm was appointed to the see, which was held by the Angles till 802. We have no record of the circumstances of this settlement except what we gather from the Whithorn monument (Fig. 5). This, however, tells us much. It bears the same Galloway Chrismon, later and further developed, and the words '[L]oc[us] Sti. Petri Apustoli', as much as to say, the old place of St Martin and St

2

Ninian is now the place of St Peter the Apostle; it has been reformed and brought into line with the Anglo-Roman church of St Wilfrid and the Synod of Whitby.

At Whitby (A.D. 664) the claim of the Doorkeeper of Heaven, new to the Columban-bred king Oswiu, decided Northumbria to accept Roman usages as against the practice of the Gaelic missionaries, and all Northumbria was Romanized. The new doctrines and the accompanying regard for St Peter spread to neighbouring countries, but slowly. In 715, as Bede tells us, Iona accepted them. In or before 716 a stone in Ireland was inscribed to St Peter (Prof. Baldwin Brown, 'Arts of Early England', V, 52). In 717 King Nechtan expelled the Columbans from his realm of Pictish Scotland, and long before this, Anglian Galloway must have made the change. It must have come about in the later years of the seventh century. And that it was not a violent change is shown by the retention of the old local symbol on a monument set up to record new conditions. If the Angles had made their reforms with the strong hand, and if they had already been accustomed to set up crosses like that of Bewcastle, they would have left a monument here very different from this rudimentary pillar.

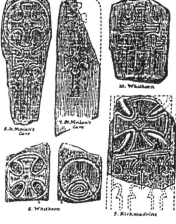

Though it anticipates the history, to see what kind of slabs and crosses the Angles actually left in Galloway, we can turn to the next group of illustrations. Figs. 6 and 7, from St Ninian's Cave; 8, a fragment at Whithorn; 9, a slab at Kirkmadrine, and 10, another at Whithorn, all bear crosses of a form distinctly Anglian of the ninth century, and even later—forms we shall meet often in the course of this study. Fig. 11 shows four sides of a cross-shaft at Whithorn; on this, side *a* has the usual pair of saints, ill drawn but characteristic; side *b* the double twist seen, for example, at Leeds; side *c* an unfinished sketch

FIGURES 6-11

for a plait, such as may be found at Ilkley Museum similarly unfinished; and the double ring-twist on *a* suggests a date as late as the tenth century, showing that even then the Anglian clerics kept their place in Galloway. That they did so we gather from the story of St Cuthbert's relics and how they found a resting-place for a time at Whithorn in 875 or later—a friendly house of Anglian affinities, far away from the area of Danish invasion. These stones show that the Angles came and stayed; but at their first coming,

3

their earliest monument (Fig. 5) was an almost timid innovation on the old traditional type. It is true that it has a dowel-hole in the top, and therefore may at one time have carried a head; but as a shaft it is merely a rude pillar, or at most, roughly hewed, like the latest of the Kirkmadrine three, and as unlike Bewcastle cross as possible.

Another point ought to be remarked in connexion with this St Peter stone. Most of the monuments we shall have in review, when they are inscribed, state plainly that they are gravestones; but this one is not. We shall come to a few others, apparently memorials of something other than an interment beneath them. Generally speaking, in the pre-Norman period we have no indication of the use of carefully carved stones as boundary-crosses, or 'preaching-crosses', still less as market-crosses; but the Roman emperors erected pillars to commemorate events, and the Northumbrians, who were not ignorant of Roman history, may have carried on that custom of marking what they considered memorable. Indeed, the custom is much more ancient, and every Anglian cleric must have known how Jacob awaked out of his sleep and took the stone that he had put for his pillows and set it up for a pillar, and called the name of that place Beth-el.

This St Peter stone, then, shows what Angles in Galloway considered suitable as a monument about the time of St Cuthbert and King Ecgfrith. In Galloway they were somewhat removed from their centres of culture, and perhaps it may be said that this work was rude for that reason, or intentionally reminiscent of local type. But we have still to find anything which can be assigned to an earlier date—anything in the way of a tall cross. What they could do in figure-sketching we see in St Cuthbert's coffin; their work in various kinds of design and decoration of metal-work was already well advanced; the architectural details of St Wilfrid's building we shall notice later; but the question now before us is that of tall stone crosses. Had they already conceived an idea of these, or is the beginning not to be found in an evolution from the rude stone pillars of Galloway through this St Peter stone?

Chapter II. Staff-Roods

ADAMNAN of Iona, writing between 692 and 697, and describing the island as it was at the time of St Columba, who died in 597, has nothing to say about stone monuments. He mentions two or three crosses but describes only one, set up to mark the place where the patron saint sat down on his last walk and said farewell to the old white horse. That cross was 'molari infixa lapidi' — stuck in a quern. It was much later that there was a mill at Iona, and in Adamnan's day the monks ground their corn in hand-mills, as we gather from the incident of Lugbeus Mocumin (Vita S. C., i, 28). Now a cross that would stand in a quern must have been a slender thing of wood. May we call it, for short, a 'staff-rood'?

Oswald, afterwards king and saint, must have known that same cross if, as Bede indicates (Hist. Eccl. ii, 3), he was educated at Iona. When he came to Northumberland in 635 he set up for his standard before the battle of Heavenfield a wooden cross. It was made in haste but heavy enough to need some trouble in fixing (*ibid.* ii, 2); 'The king himself held it with both hands until it was set fast by throwing in the earth.' Nearly a hundred years later people still cut chips from it and used them as medicine; the water in which they were soaked cured the sicknesses of themselves and their cattle.

To set up a cross where no church was and so hallow the spot is a common incident in the lives of saints. For instance, Jocelyn of Furness relates that St Kentigern did so at Crosfeld or Crosthwaite near Keswick, when he preached to the villagers. Jocelyn derives the name of the place from this tradition—whether real or fictitious we need not debate, for it is only one example of a wide-spread usage about which there can be no doubt. The doubt comes in when we are are told that an elaborately carved stone monument at Whalley was set up by St Paulinus as his preaching-cross: a missionary would not wait, even if he had the means, for such a work before delivering his message. He would set up his walking-stick with its crossed head, or cut a sapling and make a staff-rood in ten minutes.

When we read that the pilgrims who rescued St Cuthbert's relics from the Danes in 875 carried with them the cross of bishop Æthelwold (he died in 740), and when we remember their difficult and adventurous journey, especially homewards through the land of Kirkcudbright, it is difficult to believe that this was a stone cross. It is said to have been broken at the raid of 793 and mended with lead, which would apply to fixing a dowel in stone; but still the same might be done with a wooden shaft, or a sheet-lead bandage might have been nailed over the fracture. The cross was set up again at Durham in 994, more than two hundred years after it was made, and this again suggests stone, though a piece of oak would last as long as that. It has now disappeared, and as Dr Greenwell said (Durham Cath. Lib. Cat. p. 74 f.) the tradition, or supposition, that pointed out a certain cross there as Æthelwold's is entirely untenable. If it were a staff-

5

rood of some sort, the story becomes explicable. But were there staff-roods over graves?

From a large number of stone crosses, obviously reproducing the type of wooden construction, it seems certain that there were such things in common use, from at least the middle of the Anglian period (about 800) to the eleventh century. Otherwise we cannot account for the forms of which we now give a few examples, that is to say cylindrical shafts with their upper parts shaved off into four flat sides. Most of them are ornamented; that the real staff-roods were carved over with patterns is likely, because we know that wood-carving was a practice much in use during all that period. But the general idea of the round-shafted crosses is against ornamenting them in the lower part; the tree trunk is left bare, and the shaved faces are patterned.

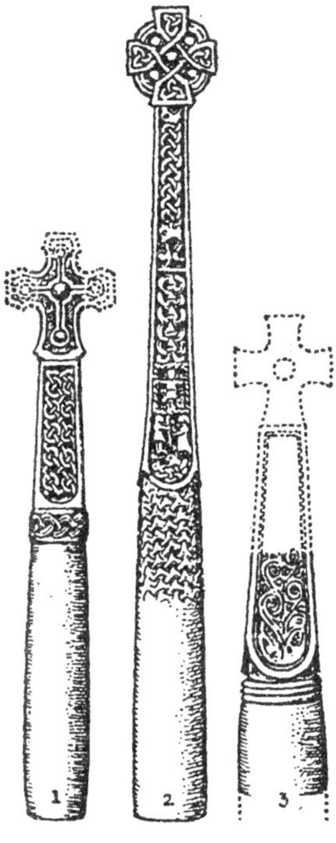

Fig. 12 (1) is the eastern one of two similar crosses at the Giant's Grave, Penrith. This cross is to be dated after the middle of the tenth century, and its companion cross about the end of that century. The band half-way up seems to suggest a sheath or binding for strengthening the post. The spine-and-boss cross-head (on which, as a wide-spread type, we have more to say in Chapter IX) looks like a cut-out cross *appliqué* or fixed with nails to the wooden head. At any rate the whole shape is not that of a round column in stone, or of the square or oblong-sectioned shaft like a gate-post trimmed as usual to form a cross. It is a staff-rood imitated in stone.

Fig. 12 (2) is the famous Gosforth (Cumberland) cross of about 1000, and (3) one of the round-shafted monuments at St Bridget's, Beckermet (Cumberland) — the one which bears on the other side the inscription which has so far puzzled interpreters. It is however pretty certainly of the eleventh century; and though only a fragment, its restoration is obvious.

FIGURE 12

In the next group Fig. 13 (4) is the 'Apostles' shaft at Collingham. The lower part is lost, but the cable-edging of the upper flat faces splits as it goes down to accommodate itself to the cylinder. This is a distinctly pre-Danish monument; it may date soon after 800; and the figures of saints contribute to justify the interpretation here put upon the next two examples. Of these Fig. 13 (5) is the Masham pillar, restored with the fragment of a very large cross-head at the same place; and Fig. 13 (6) is the suggestion made for a restoration of various pieces at Dewsbury, probably representing a

6

great 'Paulinus' Cross, known to have existed there in the time of Henry VIII. The animals and figures of the Masham shaft are of the best Anglian work; on the highest tier are Our Lord and the Apostles; below them two tiers of illustrations from the life of a saint, possibly St Cuthbert; and below is a series of animal forms gracefully though fancifully drawn. The column can hardly have been an architectural feature, but as the foot of a round-shafted cross, more ambitious than the Collingham shaft, and carrying a large head represented by the fragment still in evidence, its meaning is cleared up. For the restoration of the Paulinus cross at Dewsbury we have convincing data. A number of pieces, which could only find a place on a cylindrical column, suggest something like the Masham shaft. Of these pieces one shows the junction of the round shaft with the upper flat panels, including the 'swag' which finishes them below as at Gosforth. Higher up the cross are figure-subjects in the same style of drawing and carving as those below; the Miracle of the Loaves and Fishes, the Miracle of Cana, and adjacent to the scroll-panel over the last a Madonna and Child (not seen in this view but given in Fig. 91). The peculiar cable-edging shows that all these fragments belong to one monument. Over the scroll-panel are the feet of two figures which must have filled a panel bringing the shaft up to the size required to meet a head of which the angel and votary formed the topmost arm. The restoration

FIGURE 13

therefore is not fanciful, but built up from careful measurements and the consideration of

7

details*, and the analogies of style point to the period before the Danish invasion of 867, after which ambitious work of this kind would have been impracticable in Yorkshire.

From these we return to smaller and simpler examples in Fig. 13 (7), restored from fragments at Gilling West, and Fig. 13 (8), a late tenth or early eleventh century cross, of which enough to justify the drawing remains at Stanwick in the North Riding. Fig. 14 (9) is the stone at Ilam, Staffs., complete except for the tips of the cross-arms and the lower part of the shaft. Fig. 14 (10) the tall monument at Leek, with the triangular patch of ornament below the belt, as at Stanwick, dates A.D. 1000 or later. In

Fig. 14 (11) an attempt is made to restore the Disley (Cheshire) cross, and Fig. 14 (12) shows a little monument found in 1919 at Brailsford in Derbyshire, with an interesting figure of a warrior of the Viking Age on the shaft.

These twelve are only a selection of the instances we could give to prove that all through the pre-Norman age stone crosses were made on the lines of what we have called staff-roods. From these examples we seem to have good reason to infer the existence of the staff-rood as a common object all through that period; they give its normal form. It would be possible, however, to make a cross of a tree-trunk split down its length, showing a semicircular section; and that may be the explanation of the late Anglian relic of that form at Kirkby Stephen (Westmd.), otherwise incomprehensible (Fig. 15).

It may be pertinent to remark as a possible survival of wooden construction the boss on the cross-head, usually on one side only, and always a nuisance to the stone-carver, who has to sink a

FIGURE 14

large surface to allow for it. Considered as the head of the nail which held the transverse arm in its mortice, it becomes part of the original construction. And if, as remarked above, the apparently *appliqué* crosslet, seen in Fig. 12 (1), 13 (7), and 14 (9), and in a great number of instances besides (Fig. 116) was really an imitation of something nailed upon a wooden monument—and it is hard to see what else it could be—its five bosses explain themselves. In some late heads there is a group of bosses at the centre of the cross, as if it had been found that one big nail was not enough to keep the transom

*A model to scale can be seen in the Tolson Museum at Huddersfield, and a fuller description in *Handbook* 2 of that museum. Part of another round-shafted cross, with interlaced ornament, is at Bedale church.

straight and stiff, as any amateur carpenter would guess. And further, in the next chapter we shall see (Fig. 16a) the image of a piked staff-rood carved in stone and known by its alpenstock-point. This is surely what may be called the missing link in the evolution.

But we have not yet found the origin of the ordinary type of stone cross, that with a rectangular section, or any link between the rough stone pillar of St Peter at Whithorn, and the fully developed Anglian monument. We must try back and consider a group which is usually thought to precede the tall crosses in historical development.

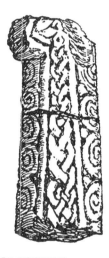

FIGURE 15. KIRKBY STEPHEN

Chapter III. Crossed Slabs

IN 'The Arts of Early England' (v. chap. 3) Professor Baldwin Brown has dealt with the Clonmacnois crossed slabs, following Professor Macalister's dating, in a way which makes it unnecessary to give details here. It is enough to remark that this Irish series is most valuable as giving a few fixed points regarding the introduction of ornament into a class of which the earlier examples are simply inscriptions with plain crosses. Key-patterns appear first on Clonmacnois slabs of about 890 and 950, and interlaced *triquetrae* first on a stone of 994. There is no doubt that such patterns were known earlier, but it does not follow that a device used in book-illumination was at the same time used in stone-carving. Invention consists in applying known formulae to new uses. One can imagine a carver saying, 'Of course I know how to draw a plait, but it would not do in stone.' And this would go on until some daring craftsman actually did it in stone.

Now if all the while such work had been done here in England, why not in Ireland? Intercourse was fairly frequent long after the Columbans had forsaken Northumbria. Bede tells us so (*Hist. Eccl.* iii, 27; iv, 4, 13; v, 9, 15, 22) and there were Saxon bishops of Mayo down to 787 (the list is in Searle, 'A. S. Bishops and Kings', 158). More than that, the crosses on Hartlepool and Lindisfarne slabs are 'Celtic' in form, unlike those on the tall monuments; which does not mean that the English borrowed the form from the Irish, nor vice versa, but that the same form was used by both, on slabs though not on tall crosses, which will be described in Chapter IX.

At first sight it looks as though English and Irish slabs were contemporaneous and their progress concurrent. Against this is the consideration that Hartlepool, as an abbey, was abandoned in 800 and Lindisfarne in 875; so that it is natural to give an earlier date to the slabs found there. But a more detailed knowledge of the abbey-sites throws a doubt on this argument. For example, at Hexham, which was certainly burnt by the Danes in 875 and a ruin all through the tenth century, not restored until about 1080, we find several crosses which cannot be pre-Danish or Anglo-Norman (for details see Chapter V); they must be the memorials of burial at the ruined site simply because it was hallowed by associations, and not because there was then a church in working order at St Wilfrid's old foundation. The same habit of clinging to an ancient though ruined church, for purposes of burial only, is so common in Scotland, even up to this day, that there is no need to labour the point. In England, to give one example, interments used to be made until the early nineteenth century at St Laurence's chapel between Workington and Cockermouth, long after the desecration of the site, and when all its history had been entirely forgotten. So on such very hallowed ground as Lindisfarne and Hartlepool, Jarrow and Monkwearmouth, it did not need an abbey with monks in residence, or even a church with divine service daily performed, to attract burials. It was enough that the dead were laid there among their ancestors and side by side with the saints in whose company they hoped to rise again.

The gravestones at these places need not therefore be pre-Danish. They may be of any age except the twelve years following the first invasion, when the Danes had not yet settled down under their Christian king Guthred. And the intercourse between Ireland and the north of England became more intimate under the kings of York, Danish and Norse, who ruled both realms up to about 954. In this intercourse we find the

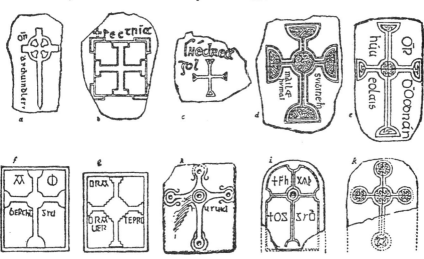

FIGURE 16

reason for the 'Celtic' crosses of the slabs better explained than as work of the Columbans before the Synod of Whitby. Indeed it is not known that the Columbans made any stone monuments so early.

A few of the well-known slabs are sketched (Fig. 16) to illustrate the series. Clonmacnois *a* is hesitatingly attributed to the Cuindles who died in 720; if that is the date of the stone, it is an early example of the wheel-cross, and as the stem ends in a spike it may represent a 'staff-rood' meant to be stuck in the ground or used as a walking-stick.

Fig. 16 *b* bears the name of Rectnia or Reachtnia, whose death as abbot of the place is recorded by the Four Masters in 779 (true date 784). Snedriagal, the next abbot, died 781 (true date 786), and his stone (*c*) is a very plain cross. About 890 is the date given for Suibne mac Maile Humai (*d*); his cross has key-pattern in the semicircles at the ends of the arms and 'Late-Celtic' curves in the centre. In 994 died Odhran

Ua h-Eolais, scribe of Clonmacnois, who is commemorated with a cross (*e*) having *triquetrae* in the centre and on the arm-ends.

The three following are from Hartlepool. With the simplest (*f*) compare the form of Suibne's cross, and this is the usual Hartlepool shape; the lettering, however, has a rather early appearance and this example may be pre-Danish. The next (*g*) is unique in its stepped outline to the cross; the stone (in the British Museum) is much worn, but earlier antiquaries read it, 'Orate pro Ediluini. Orate pro Uermund & Torhtsuid', with the last *d* crossed to express an aspirate (*dh*). Now the evidence of coins seems to indicate that the crossed *d* came into use in the ninth century; Ecgfrith (670-685) and Aldfrith (685-705) are written with a D at the end; Æthelred I (ceased to reign in 796) is spelt EDILRED; but Æthelred II (841-850) has the crossed D to represent *th*. Another point with regard to the inscription is that it mentions together Vermund (a man's name) and Torhtsuith (a woman's) who are—curiously enough—also given on a separate stone, while Ethelwini is also separately mentioned. But if these burials were of monks and nuns in an abbey, why should a man and woman be buried together in the same grave and named on the same stone? If they were husband and wife the interments were of secular persons, and the possibility of their later date is increased. The third here drawn from Hartlepool (*h*) shows the nearest approach in that series to ornamentation; the name is mutilated.

At Lindisfarne a number of small grave-slabs have been found recently and are illustrated by Mr C. R. Peers in *Archaeologia*, vol.74 (1925). Two of the older-known examples are enough to show what the series is like. Fig. 16 *i*, inscribed with runes and in what is called Hiberno-Saxon letters 'Osgyth', the *d* crossed to form a *dh*, is therefore perhaps not very early. The cross is of the same form as that of Berchtgyd at Hartlepool and of the two later Clonmacnois examples. And *k* has the same ornament as *e* at Clonmacnois. Taking these all together it is difficult to believe that they are not contemporary in their process of development from simpler to more ornamented forms.

Though Hartlepool and Lindisfarne furnish the largest groups, small slabs—whether 'pillow-stones' or otherwise intended—are not uncommon. As examples of such, take the stone found at Hexham and inscribed 'Tundwini' on the arms of the cross (Fig. 17 *a*); the two at Wensley, one to Donfrid (*b*) with birds of the late Anglian style in the spandrils, and the other to Eadberehct (*c*) with a similar cross of Anglian form. Much later than these is that from Monkwearmouth (in the British Museum) inscribed in runes 'Tidfirth' (*d*), the form of the name showing the tenth century, and the rude figures quite unlike the graceful if unnatural shapes on Donfrid's stone. It is impossible that this should be the bishop Tidfrith of Hexham who died in 821, for it is at least a hundred years later. The Warkworth example (*e*) is evidently a headstone; its 'Celtic' cross connects it with a number in the north-east of England where, as at Hartlepool and Lindisfarne, that form of cross prevailed over the usual Anglian. At West Witton in Wensleydale is a small slab (*f*) with elaborate late ninth century plaits; a near neighbour to the slabs at Wensley. One of two small slabs at Lythe (*g*) is shown because they occur in a group of late monuments, and may be rude rather than early. They seem to be examples of an unpretending type of monument, not much ruder than the slab (*h*) at Birtley on the North Tyne. From Bothal (in the Blackgate Museum, Newcastle) are two round-headed stones (one sketched as *i*) which might possibly be parts of wheel-crosses, but are more likely to be headstones such as we have seen from Warkworth, not far away. And finally, in this group, an example at Adel (near Leeds) is sketched (*k*) to show a headstone of 1100 or later, with the rustication which took the place of true interlacing, when the untrained carvers of the overlap between pre-

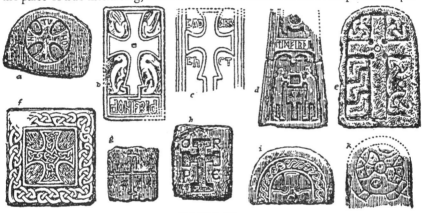

FIGURE 17

Norman and Norman art had forgotten their trade, and the public had forgotten its taste. In these we see a transition from the 'pillow-stone' or earlier small slab to the ordinary headstone of a later age.

Taking a hasty tour round the Celtic regions of Britain we may note—though it is not necessary to illustrate—a few small crossed slabs, merely to show that such things were not confined to narrow limits. At St Andrews (Fife) are four ('Early Christian Monuments of Scotland', Figs. 375, 557-559) with 'Late-Celtic' in the spandrils of crosses that might be Northumbrian in shape; at Papa Stronsay (*ibid*. Fig. 21) an ornamental cross with 'dne di' in minuscules above it; at Logie Coldstone, Aberdeen, a small slab with a free-armed Celtic cross in relief (*ibid*. Fig. 213), resembling the water-worn boulders at Iona, one of which (*ibid*. Fig. 424) has a wheel-cross in relief. The slabs of Iona (*ibid*. Figs. 401, 402, 405, 406, 414-417) hardly come into the list we are now dealing with, being more like grave-covers; but they shew forms of Celtic crosses varying from Mailfataric's plain, small and early slab, now at Inverary, to interlaced examples which belong to the restored Iona of the tenth

13

century. At Eileach-Naiomh, Columba's Hinba, still stands, or stood not long ago, a headstone with a plain Latin cross incised, and there is another from the same island at the National Museum of Antiquities, Edinburgh (*ibid.* Fig. 420) with one like it from Eilean Mòr (*ibid.* Fig. 419); the type is simple, but in such circumstances the date is very uncertain—though hardly that of St Columba's mother, as tradition says of the Eileach-Naiomh stone.

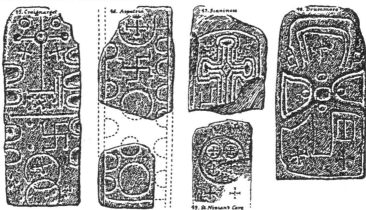

FIGURE 18

At St Ninian's Cave, near Whithorn, are several crossed slabs which seem to range, by the shape of their crosslets, with stones of the Viking age, such as the slab from Sinniness (Fig. 18) on the same coast and that from Drummore across Luce Bay, both now at Edinburgh. The Sinniness stone has a bit left of a T丄T pattern, showing that it is of the tenth century or later, and the Drummore cross, with its book under the sinister arm, is evidently late. The Craignarget slab (Fig. 18), found near Sinniness and now at Edinburgh, is placed in the drawing beside fragments of one at Aspatria, Cumberland. Both are marked with the *swastika* or *gammadion*, a form of cross which the Northmen must have learnt on their early journeys through Russia to Byzantium, just as they picked up their first word for a Christian priest—*papi*—from that source. This suggests a tenth century date, for that was the time when Viking settlers were only half Christianized; a little later they seem to have adopted, with modifications, the art of the Angles among whom they settled in Galloway and Cumberland. In the same group is drawn one of the slabs from St Ninian's Cave near Whithorn, with crosslets like the others, and perhaps contemporary.

In the Isle of Man many small crossed slabs are known. Mr Kermode in his 'Manx Crosses' gives (plate VI) a couple of headstones like those of Eileach-Naiomh, and a crossed boulder somewhat resembling the Logie Coldstone and Iona boulders, perhaps

14

pillow-stones. From these he goes on (Plate VII and following) to a great variety of small headstones and slabs, some of which have 'Celtic' crosses, some of Anglian form; they might range from the ninth to the eleventh century. And in Wales we find a round-topped headstone with a wheel-cross, at Nefyn (Westwood, 'Lapidarium Walliae', plate 83), and a little slab at Merthyr Mawr (*ibid.* plate 29) very like the Birtley stone without its inscription. Westwood assigns this to the twelfth century; the second stone (*ibid.* Fig. 4) at the same place is certainly late as indicated by its plaits.

This short review suggests that small slabs, pillow-stones and head-stones, varying in local style, were usual over a wide area; and in general they run on from pre-Danish times through the Viking Age to the twelfth century. Their simpler forms were a cheap kind of stone monument, but perhaps out of this type was evolved the ampler grave-cover. In Northumbria we find a number of examples, and can argue to more. For instance, the rock-cut graves at Heysham, near Lancaster, of course had covers, and they are late tenth to early eleventh century, because the chapel of St Patrick which stands near them must be the tenth century building of a Christian Northman from Ireland.*

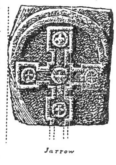

Jarrow

Monkwearmouth.

FIGURE 19

The larger cross-slabs at Jarrow and Monkwearmouth (Fig. 19) are in bold relief, unsuited to lying flat; they would catch the dirt in their hollows, their relief would be abraded, and they would soon be defaced. They may have been upright headstones, but the question is not important for our present purpose. They are figured here to show the shapes of their crosses, ranging them with the smaller slabs we have already examined. Bishop Browne has remarked that the name of Hereberecht has been added to a readymade stone ('Notes on . . . Monkwearmouth', 12); and this means that the type was common and that the 'Celtic' cross was in use in Northumbria at Anglian sites and with Anglian inscriptions. And as the tall crosses which we have yet to discuss were certainly contemporary, but show no such 'Celtic' shapes, it follows that

*The history of Heysham is shortly this: an Anglian wooden church of the eighth or ninth century to St Peter, with the ninth century stone. This church being decayed, Norse settlers from Ireland in the tenth century built, with local Anglian help, the chapel to St Patrick, and cut these rock-graves, also the hogback in the eleventh century. A stone church to St Peter on the old site was built before 1094, when it is mentioned; and rebuilt in the twelfth century. The fancies about St Patrick's visit need not be taken seriously.

15

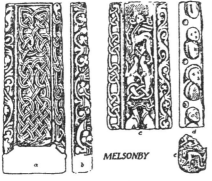

MELSONBY

FIGURE 20

slab-cutting was a separate art with its own methods and traditions.* Of such departmental limitations we have plenty of evidence in the later middle ages, when a miniaturist, for example, was not allowed to paint large pictures and every craftsman had to 'stick to his last'. But it is impossible to crowd all the English slabs we have reviewed into one early Columban period; they cannot have been made before 664, when similar Irish forms go on to 994. Crossed slabs must have been in use concurrently with staff-roods and tall stone crosses throughout the whole pre-Norman age.

In this connexion it remains only to mention a few graveslabs and recumbent monuments of Anglian and Anglo-Viking character. Many of them are short of the length of a normal man or woman, but the same can be said of the ordinary medieval grave-slab, and perhaps they were not intended to seal the grave but only to lie on the top of the stones that actually covered it in. Much would depend on the means for getting a piece of stone large enough, and it

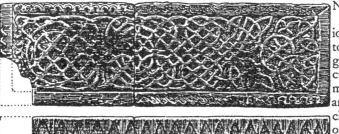

KIRKDALE f.
FIGURE 21

KIRKDALE

FIGURE 22

*Any practical draughtsman who is familiar with the crosses knows that they were drawn free-hand on the stone before carving: e.g. a horizontal line very frequently curves a little, and in a pattern that allows it the member opposite the designer's right hand is usually a little higher than it ought to be in strict symmetry. Cross-carvers did not lay out their detail geometrically. But slab-carvers did; they used rule and compass in all but the rudest kind of work.

16

must be remembered that, although some churches in the pre-Norman age were built of masonry, most were of wood, and the quarryman's craft was practically unknown except at a few important centres.

Forming a step in the tower-stair at Filey church is a fragment of regular Anglian plait-work (Fig. 26 c) which may be ninth century, and as it must have tapered slightly was perhaps a grave-cover.

Melsonby in the North Riding possesses two recumbent grave-stones, one (Fig. 20 *ab*) only 33 inches long, with late Anglian plaits and scrolls. The other (Fig. 20 *cd*) cut down so that its length is not known, is remarkable for its late Anglian beasts, and the curious row of human heads emerging from holes on its vertical side (compare stones given later from Hoddam and Heysham) ; its plait and scroll are of the ninth century.

At Kirkdale church between Helmsley and Pickering there are two fine slabs, one popularly ascribed to Bishop Cedd (Fig. 21) and the other to King Ethelwald (Fig. 22). The first is 67½in. long, and bears a plait with rings, a type at least three hundred years later than the bishop.* The other has a 'Celtic' cross with late Anglian scrolls, and is a hundred years later than the king, who was deposed in 765, and was probably dead in 774 when his son was on the throne.

At Thornhill church (West Riding) are fragments which we venture to restore as in Fig. 23. Father Haigh thought that this was the monument of King Osberht, killed by the Danes at York, March 21st, 867; and indeed the stone may be of that date, though Osberht was not an unusual name.

At York, St Mary Bishophill senior, is a slab (figured in the Yorks. Archæol. Journal, xx, 206) 47½ inches long and slightly coffin-shaped with a straight-lined 'patriarchal' cross, plaits with rings and a double-cable edging. The knot at the base on the dexter side has been bungled, and the whole is mid-eleventh century work. In the Hospitium (No. 7) at the Philosophical Society's museum is a somewhat similar slab from St Denis (Fig. 24) with the plaits ending in dragon-heads and the strands bifurcated, meaning the tenth or more likely eleventh century. From the same church in the same collection is also the interesting coped stone, 43¾ inches long (Fig. 25) carved with a Noah's

* For the discussion of the relative ages of running patterns see Chapter VIII.

FIG. 23

FIG. 24

ark-full of animals of Scando-Celtic character, some having the joint-spiral which marks that class of design. The crest on the top of the dexter side (as shown in the drawing) is distinctly eleventh century.

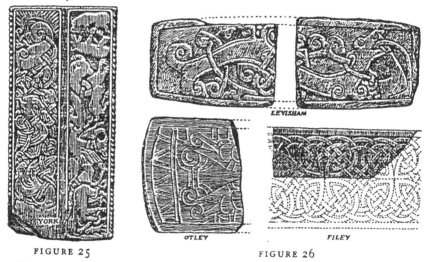

FIGURE 25   FIGURE 26

Likewise Scandinavian is the slab at Levisham, north of Pickering (Fig. 26 a), with its dragon of the tenth-eleventh century. This restored would still be less than four feet long, but its coffin shape makes it obviously a grave-cover.

At Otley church is the interesting fragment of grave-slab (Fig. 26 b) in the Scandinavian style which dates it early eleventh century, like slabs in the British Museum from London. Finally, and towards the end of the book, we illustrate the Birstall fragment (Fig. 224) to show the last efforts of debased pre-Norman art in its clumsy, thoughtless imitation of key-pattern; this, no doubt, is of the overlap into Norman, about the beginning of the twelfth century. And having sketched the general course of art-progress and decadence in the separate and minor department of slabs, we can turn our attention to the tall crosses.

18

Chapter IV. The Northumbrians & their Crosses

BEFORE attempting the discussion of the tall crosses it is desirable to be clear as to the people for whom and perhaps by whom they were made. We will not beg the question by saying that Northumbrians carved the Bewcastle cross, for it is usual, especially among foreign writers, to regard the race as barbarous, and to express wonder or doubt that any native Englishman could have had a hand in work of an artistic character. Much is to said for this view; but in the first place, has not the artistic value of pre-Norman cross-carving been rather exaggerated by admiring antiquaries? Its interest is undeniable, but as design and execution it rises only here and there above a very moderate standard. Some of the most famous crosses show downright bad work in parts; the Magdalen of the Ruthwell cross could hardly be worse, and as stone-carving the whole of the Bewcastle cross is elementary. One great asset of the series is its variety. Though we have seen that the slabs were ready-made we cannot charge the crosses with being turned out to trade patterns, like the monuments of a modern churchyard. They are experimental and ingenious, sometimes pretty. They are fair amateurs' work as a whole.

In the second place, were the English of Bede and Alcuin so barbarous as they look to hasty readers of history? The first Angles in Northumbria were no doubt a very rough kind of people, a rude northern race who began to come over the North Sea not before A.D. 500 and pushed up the rivers boat-load by boat-load, to look for an easier life than they had led in Slesvik or in Southern Norway. They found a country without government, undefended and almost deserted. The Roman civilization of Yorkshire had been wiped out and the old towns were overgrown with a hundred years' weeds. Some Britons still haunted their ancient homes, but not in numbers. No conquest of Yorkshire by an organized campaign was needed; stories to that effect are myths of a later age, confusing the battles of Eadward the Elder and Æthelstan with legends of King Arthur. Round York itself there are traces of early Anglian farms, but no hint that there was any city in the days when those farms were inhabited. About 550 other Angles settled on the coast of Northumberland, and gradually the scattered groups coalesced and foregathered into two kingdoms, Deira in Yorkshire and Bernicia round about Bamborough. By about 600 they were fairly wide-spread, according to Professor Ekwall's analysis of the place-names ('English Place-names in -ing'; Lund and Oxford, 1923) which shows that the -ings and -inghams cannot be much later; and these are dotted all over the map of northern England, with a gap in the present county of Durham where, for the time, a borderland divided the two realms. This fringe was inhabited, a the place-names show, by Britons.

Some day, it is to be hoped, exploration will discover the early abodes of these sixth century Angles and tell us the kind of life they led. Meanwhile we can only infer it from such remains as have been found in Saxon huts, earlier by half a century, in Berkshire, described by Mr Thurlow Leeds in 'Archaeologia', vol. 73 (1923). These huts, a dozen in a row and perhaps more in the whole village, were each under 20 feet in length, very rudely put together of posts filled in with walls of mud and straw (not wattle and daub) and highly irregular in plan. The floors in some cases seem to have been flagged, and in them were pits for storing grain and for cooking, which was done by boiling up a clay pot with hot stones. In some huts they made these pots and carried on the work of smiths; their other industries are represented by spinning-whorls and weaving-tools and by a cow-bell, which shows (what otherwise can be inferred) that the people lived a pastoral life, not that of warriors pillaging a rich country and enjoying the proceeds of brigandage, though they used a few odds and ends found in deserted Roman villas. The sixth century Angles must have lived in the same way, rude backwoodsmen.

Now turn a page and see the seventh century Angles producing Oswald and Aldfrith, Wilfrid and Benedict Biscop, Ceolfrid and Bede. It was a rapid and startling transformation. If it could be shown that they had progressed so far as to carve or even appreciate the Bewcastle cross before the century was three-quarters past, it would be a miracle of progress. But military and political strength comes before the arts; literature usually before monumental sculpture. The impetus of Christianity explains much, and the first stone churches were built by imported architects; but it is asking the impossible to require that decorated stone crosses, a 'luxury-trade', should have originated so soon out of a rude and comparatively artless stage. Wood-carving and metal-work on a small scale, and with some degree of taste, they no doubt used; but the step from these minor crafts to the Bewcastle cross is a long one. Even if the work was done by foreigners, we have to ask 'where was the public that wanted it, and paid for it?' We need a little more time for the evolution.

Even so, the advance to the age of Alcuin is remarkable. The Anglian boor had it in him to show some political and fighting capacity; and that he had a feeling for poetry is proved by his Beowulf and his Cædmon, not to mention many a story in Bede indicating as much. But aptitude for plastic art is often the result of a mixture of races, especially when a strong and energetic stock is crossed with one that inherits some artistic instinct, and that is exactly the case of the Northumbrians. Bede's contemporaries were not pure-bred Angles. They had absorbed the Britons whose presence among them is attested by place-names and by various waifs and strays of historical information, which entirely forbid the idea that the new-comers exterminated the natives. The intercourse between Angles and Celts must have been greatly increased when Oswald came back from Scotland in 634 with his Celtic comrades and introduced the Columban clergy. In the next generation King Oswiu's first wife was a British princess from Strathclyde; and his brother married a Pictish princess whose son, by the rules of matriarchate in vogue among the Picts, became their king. What royalty does recommends itself to the people at large, and that royalty did it proves an absence of the racial animosity which used to be taken for granted.

Now what can we gather about the Britons, left over from the Roman period and from the Pictish and Scottish devastations in the north of England? Were they savages who painted themselves blue and ran naked in the woods? From explorations of 'British settlements' we know that in the later years of Roman government, attested by coin-finds, some of the most rustic lived in homesteads walled around with massive stone or earthen ramparts, in stone houses usually circular—the 'beehive huts' of the Celtic countries but not always small huts. At Ewe Close near Crosbyravensworth in Westmorland and at Stone Walls near Urswick in Furness, the main houses of the groups were found to be fifty feet wide. The people were agricultural and pastoral; they used Roman pottery and metal-work; and in or near some of these places very considerable hoards of Roman coins have been found. That this civilisation lasted until the coming of the Angles is shown by such place-names as Walton, by which the Angles themselves knew the abodes of their 'Welsh' neighbours, as at Cartmel, which was given, 'with the Britons there' to St Cuthbert in or before 685. And in that year, when St Cuthbert visited Carlisle, already Anglian, the people of the place showed him their Roman antiquities and used the Roman-British name of the town, arguing a continuance of history impossible unless British population had survived. Those Britons were the descendants of the Romanized Britons of the fourth century, and though diminished in numbers and reduced in circumstances by foreign invasions they were the same as those who had carved the Corstopitum lion and the goddesses of Coventina's Well at Carrawburgh on the Wall. We do not suggest that the lion is as good as Greek art, nor the goddesses equal to the best Roman; but a race that had learned so much and had been trained for three hundred years by Roman teachers could not have lost all its inheritance in four or five generations.

In the mixture of these Britons with the sturdy Anglian boors we find the beginnings of the English of the seventh century, ready to receive the teaching of Gaul and Italy through Wilfrid and his contemporaries. And the district where that teaching first took root — Hexham, Jarrow and Monkwearmouth — is precisely the area where the British element was strongest, where British place-names survive between Anglian Deira and Bernicia, in the country remembered to the end of the tenth century by the writer of the Life of St Oswald as forest land. The Britons, left alone, produced no art worthy of the name in Wales before the Viking Age. The Old Saxons, left alone, were still barbarous when the Northumbrians sent missions to them. But the two races commingled created a great nation of which the centre and focus was this land between Tees and Tyne.

In 678 they had not yet risen to an interest in sculptured ornament. This we know from the fact that carved stones from Corstopitum were used by Wilfrid's masons as mere building material. The fine Roman horseman, now to be seen in Hexham Church, was discovered in one of the foundation walls of Wilfrid's fabric. The decorative slab now displayed on the north wall (Fig. 27) was built into the crypt. The 'Archer' slab (Fig. 28) tentatively restored from the fragments at Hexham and Durham appears to be derived from

HEXHAM: from the Crypt, 1908.

FIGURE 27

the Roman Ara Pacis style and to have been also from Corstopitum. The place where it was found in the church is unrecorded; we do not know that it was used as ornament there, but though crosses show leaf-scrolls, figures and birds, this stone never served as a model for any Anglian design. About twenty years later (if 698 is the true date of St Cuthbert's coffin) we can see the local motives of ornament; hasty perhaps, in execution and in a general way foreshadowing the draughtsmanship of saints and angels as in the greater crosses, but without hint of scrolls and plaits. The Lindisfarne Gospels (assuming an early date for the illuminations) must be put on one side, for book-illustration was a separate art, and that book is the outcome of Irish influence of which we have already found indications in post-Columban Northumbria. There is no mention in Bede's 'Ecclesiastical History' up to 731 of great stone crosses, though he describes wooden and metal crosses and stone coffins and various tombs. We have no reason to believe that there was anything of the sort except the Whithorn stone to St Peter; and that, as we have seen, was imitated from the rude pillars of ancient Galloway.

Then suddenly follows a period to which we must assign a number of monuments which we call Anglian. They are distinct from Saxon or Celtic because they are found within the area occupied by the Anglian kingdom of Northumbria at its widest extension in the seventh and eighth centuries, including the south of the present Scotland as far as Whithorn and Abercorn. These crosses are also to be called Anglian as distinct from Anglo-Danish and Anglo-Norse because, at the Danish conquest beginning in 867, the greater Northumbrian abbeys disappeared and there was no further opportunity of carrying on the masons' workshops which had been in the service of the church. In some parts of the West and North, where the Danes did not settle, there was less of a break with tradition and Anglian styles were preserved, changing only gradually. But in central and eastern Yorkshire, Danish taste modified the patterns which nevertheless started from Anglian models, and in Cumberland a little later the Norse-descended settlers evolved a new style, similarly based on Anglian. All these newcomers had no masons' art of their own, on their arrival, but becoming Christians and adopting English habits they accepted the current fashion of memorial stones, probably employing at first such of the Anglian craftsmen as remained among them, though they were not of the best. So we can trace the evolution through the tenth

22

century into the eleventh by the help of known facts regarding Danish and Scandinavian art; and at the end of the eleventh century we see the dregs of the old style, changing into Norman as the twelfth century dawns.

Now of the comparative age of these later Anglo-Danish and Anglo-Norse stones we are certain by the positions in which many have been discovered, built into the foundations of twelfth century churches. Already in 1077-1088 the Abbot Paul of St Alban's could destroy the earlier monuments and call them 'rudes et idiotae'. Rather later there was a wholesale use or misuse of them when the building of stone churches became customary in the north, though in some places they were allowed to stand. They could not have been desecrated unless the families concerned had died out, and some time must have passed before this was possible. We can therefore say that the Gosforth hogbacks were certainly much older than the foundations of the mid-twelfth century church in which they were embedded. But these hogbacks are of a type developed out of earlier work, such as the late Anglian hogback at Dewsbury (Fig. 196) and that itself is obviously a late example of the Anglian scrolls which we see in monuments for which we must find a still earlier place. This process of reasoning, repeated in many various instances, gives a rough classification into strata, like geological horizons. It affords what amounts to a scientific demonstration of the general course of pre-Norman art-history, and forbids us to place, for example, the Gosforth cross in the Anglian period, or the Bewcastle cross in the twelfth century.

FIGURE 28. HEXHAM

Further, there are means of checking some points in the process. The Ormside Cup (Fig. 29; in the museum at York; fully described by Professor Baldwin Brown, op. cit. 318 ff) has been broken and mended with a patch whose details must be regarded as belonging to about the year 900, as Mr Thurlow Leeds first pointed out (Liverpool Annals of Archaeology, iv. 8). It is therefore considerably earlier than that date; and when we find the ornament of its base repeated on the Northallerton cross (Fig. 30) we feel confidence in saying that the Northallerton cross is ninth century at least. We know the kind of names in use before the tenth century, and that they were not used in the twelfth; and when we find them on stones at Hackness or Thornhill (Yorks.) we can-

23

not attribute the stones to Norman carvers. We know the language and the writing in runes and 'Hiberno-Saxon' of the Angles and also those of the tenth and eleventh centuries; this gives a position in the series to inscribed stones whose patterns and style, re-

FIGURE 29. ORMSIDE CUP

FIGURE 30

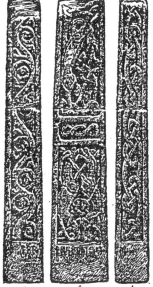

COLLINGHAM
FIGURE 31

peated on others, date these others also. In certain cases of overlap this test is not convincing to a generation or so, but the evidence for dating is cumulative, and local variations have to be taken into account. In any case, all the argument that can be brought to bear merely fixes rough limits to the period of a given stone. To attempt the equation of a name in an inscription with a known historical name is always unsafe and usually misleading; the general character of the monument shows its period, and its typology is to be trusted —the typology at which we arrive by considering the series as a whole and including all known examples in our review.

There are many lines on which this argument can be tested. Working back from examples known to be of the Anglo-Norman overlap to the later Scandinavian style

24

of the earlier part of the eleventh century; thence to examples of the first Scandinavian work, in many Yorkshire stones of the tenth century, we come to the Collingham dragon (Fig. 31 *f*, upper panel), which shows the overlap between the purer Anglian school and its modification by later feeling. The Collingham beast with its head between its forelegs is obviously a later version of the Cundall-Aldborough beast in a florid and not very early Anglian work (Fig. 32). Date the Collingham dragon late ninth century and its prototype early ninth century, and the process is apparent. Before the Cundall-Aldborough stone was possible there must have been the purer and simpler types, more nearly like those found in Italy, whence Benedict Biscop and other early patrons of ecclesiastical art drew their inspiration through the intercourse of which we have abundant evidence. That the craftsmen came straight from the East has yet to be proved, and until something more like an Anglian cross than the pillars of

CUNDALL   AND   ALDBOROUGH

FIGURE 32

Odzun* and more like an Anglian scroll than the hard unrelieved lines of Syrian design from Mschatta† can be adduced, we have not found the origin of Northumbrian crosses in Oriental sources. That a general style of scroll and plait was common in those ages throughout all Christendom is taken for granted; but the differentia of the style as seen in English work argues a native development.

What then were the circumstances which permitted a native development? We are told by some writers that Northumbria in the eighth century was barbarous, the scene

* Fig. 65 in *Origins of Christian Church Art*, by Josef Strzygowski, English translation, Oxford, 1923.

† Fig. 16 in *Early English Ornament*, by J. Bröndsted, English translation, London, 1924.

25

of discord, revolt and slaughter; fire, pestilence and famine. On the contrary, it was a land of peace and plenty, with very little in the way of external interference and that always unsuccessful; with brilliant progress and extension under King Eadberht, and such a standard of literature under his brother, archbishop Ecgberht, that Alcuin could be bred at York and invited, late in the century, by Charlemagne, to superintend the central school of Europe and furnish his library with books. In Alcuin's time, there was rivalry for the throne between two dynasties, and their retainers occasionally met and fought; but that does not mean war. It means no more than faction-fights on a much smaller scale than the Wars of the Roses during which art and learning were by no means eclipsed. The abbeys, at any rate, were undisturbed, and monumental art is ecclesiastical, carried on under the wing of the Church and in its peace. No time and no place could be more favourable for this particular development than the eighth century in Northumbria.

Towards its close the first signs of Viking activity began to show themselves, but it was not until 867 that the great Danish host appeared, attracted by the very wealth of the country. Political and military power was then on the decline, but that has coexisted in many countries with the meridian of art. We have therefore up to 867 for the rise and progress of the Anglian School of cross-carving. That it began after Bede's time (he died in 735) we have already suggested on general grounds. It remains to attempt a nearer view.

Chapter V. The School of Hexham

AT Hexham in 678 St Wilfrid's church was finished; not the first attempt in the north at stone architecture but the most striking and successful up to that time. Before that period there had been no masonry, in the sense of stone work cut ornamentally, since the Roman government deserted Northumbria. If there had been craftsmen skilled in that trade, Wilfrid and Benedict Biscop would not have needed to import their artificers.

Before 732 bishop Acca had enlarged and adorned this fabric. Bede mentions altars and arches added by him, and gives us to understand (Hist. Eccl. v. 20) that he did very much to increase the contents and effects of a church already of fine character but, we infer, not so rich as fifty years of Northumbria's growing wealth and progress since Wilfrid's day now demanded.

In 875 the church was burnt by Halfdan's Danes but, as we have seen, the ruined site was used for burials during the tenth and eleventh centuries. And about 1080-1085, Eilaf the priest restored the building.

Fragments of various periods exist at the church and it is pertinent to our subject to ask whether we can classify them enough to suggest the kind of ornament and carving that was in use at the three periods—Wilfrid's to 678, Acca's to 732 and Eilaf's to 1085. We can see without much doubt that the balusters in Fig. 33b are clumsy imita-

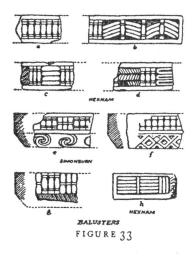

BALUSTERS

FIGURE 33

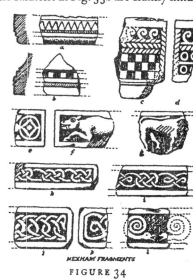

HEXHAM FRAGMENTS

FIGURE 34

27

tions of the simple but finished work of the same kind in *a, b, c, d*, and that the balusters at Simonburn (*e, f, g,*) come between the two types and belong to a period when the first 'naturalistic' intention of the motive, representing book-cupboards or what not,

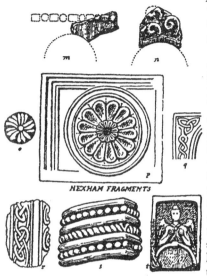

HEXHAM FRAGMENTS

FIGURE 35

was forgotten but combined with ornament such as we find elsewhere, dating from the ninth century.

In the next group of fragments (Fig. 34) *a* and *b*, timid and severe, contrast with *c* (an impost from Hexham at Durham Cathedral Library) and *e f* (certainly not the Roman Twentieth Legion's boar) and *g;* and these with the late plaits and snakes, coarsely carved, of the rest. Now the volute-crests of *c d* have already been referred by Dr Greenwell (Durham Catalogue, p. 66) to the ciborium of St George, Valpolicella, of 712, and to another at Bagnacavallo, thought to be eighth century; and we need look no farther for their date. They must be Acca's work, and in his time the chequers (here drawn from the stone; the illustration in the Durham Catalogue is indeterminate) were possible, which throws light on the Bewcastle cross. So too we have a cable, more boldly drawn than in the earlier work of *a* and *b*; but this disposes of doubts on the antiquity of the cable in crosses.

The second group of Hexham fragments (Fig. 35) gives the panel (*p*) cleared of the scabbling which defaces it and showing an early type of work, used at San Clemente, Rome (Rivoira, 'Lombardic Architecture', ii, Fig. 541), before Wilfrid's time. The roundel (*o*) is the centre of this panel enlarged; it has the naturalism of early work and may well be of the first building. The incised *triquetrae* and plait (*q*) on the so-called Frith Stool, probably the bishop's seat, must be later than 678, because the first bishop of Hexham was not consecrated until after the church was built; at any time a stone seat might be added; and the knot may be a subsequent ornament. In any case it is earlier than 821, after which there were no more Anglian bishops of Hexham. The rest of this group are of the late coarse work as in Figs. 33*h*, 34*h-l*, a couple of window-heads (*m* and *n*), a pilaster or perhaps coping of a grave-stone (*r*), a curious carinated pilaster-base (*s*) and an angel (*t*) not of the better Anglian character. What we seem to learn from these details is valuable, if we are right in classing them thus:—
(1) the timid, ineffective attempts of the seventh century masons, (2) the much bolder

28

and more accomplished eighth century work and (3) the coarse carving of the eleventh century.

Another relic of early Hexham is the Rood-figure of which there are fragments (Fig. 36). The stone is not local, and the modelling of the drapery and feet is beyond

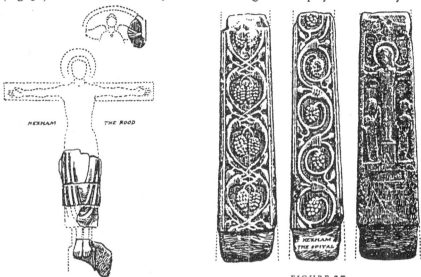

FIGURE 36

FIGURE 37

any ordinary cross-carver's powers. The long drapery is well known in early crucifixes, and the little fragment which seems to imply the wing of an angel perhaps belonged to a figure in the arches above the cross. If this was one of Acca's additions to the embellishment of the church, brought oversea from Gaul or Italy, it gives us a source for the crucifix seen on the cross-shaft at the Spital, near Hexham (Fig. 37), and for other crucifixes, as on the Ruthwell cross and in a long range of examples, increasingly decadent, throughout the ninth and tenth centuries, discussed in Chapter X.

Bishop Acca had to leave his diocese in 732, but when he died in 740 he was buried at Hexham. The twelfth century account (included in Symeon of Durham's 'Historia Regum', under the year 740) describes his tomb as known by 'two stone crosses, decorated with wonderful carving, one at the head and the other at the foot' of the grave; the cross at the head was inscribed with a statement that he was buried there. If the remains of two great crosses now at Durham (Cathedral Library, Nos. III and IV) are not identical with these it is most extraordinary, because none other is forthcoming, even in the smallest fragment, to take the place; and these answer to the description except

29

FIGURE 38. ACCA CROSS, UPPER PART.

that the name of Acca is lost, with much of the lettering on the greater shaft. What can still be read is suitable to a grave-monument of the time: — 'A[et O] ... SC ... UNIGENITO FILIO DEI...' and of the 'wonderful carving' (Figs. 38, 39) there is no doubt though so worn as to give some difficulty in following out its details with certainty. An interesting modern copy, made under the direction of Mr C. C. Hodges, stands at the entrance to Hexham cemetery: the drawing given here is made independently, without attempt to continue the pattern on the missing part. The fourth side, which has the traces of inscription, is too damaged to draw with any satisfaction. The real original height is unknown; if there were a slight entasis the sides would come together sooner than with the outline ruled straight.

Looking at the detail one is struck by its naturalism. Tendrils of vine are suggested as far as possible, and the bunches are grape-bunches. But there are very few leaves, and those not fully displayed with the shape dear to designers. One asks, 'had the carver a vine before him, or was he only working from reminiscence or description?' An Oriental or an Italian, drawing as naturalistically as this, would surely go a step further. A landscape-painter's naturalism one does not expect; to carve in stone at all, forms must be conventionalized; but the difference between this cross and still less naturalistic work will appear shortly. And it seems to be the law of art-progress that naturalism marks the nascent style, turning to more and more conventionalism as time goes on. If this cross was the first of its series, it plays the part to perfection, except for the wonder that it could have been made at the date (soon after 740) and in 'barbarous' Northumbria.

The wonder is partly explained if we consider the circumstances. Bishop Acca's work at the church must have brought to Hexham some skilled craftsmen and must have trained more. During his eight years' absence it is conceivable that they still remained there, variously employed. At his death it would be the most natural thing in the world

30

that they should put their best strength into making a memorial worthy of one of whom Bede had written, a little earlier, that he was 'great in the sight of God and man'.

Still, it is a surprising work. But the world is full of surprises, and every time an artist of genius arises there is a fresh surprise. That the designer of this cross was an artist cannot be doubted, and to such a man all things are possible — within limits. What he did was to combine the idea of the staff-rood with that of the stone pillar, and to use as ornament the scroll-work, of which his examples were found in products of the Ravenna school, by this time fairly widespread in Italy and southern France. In the museum at Arles, among fourth century Romano-Christian relics, is a marble with the double vine-scroll, showing the way to the Hexham pattern. What he did *not* was to use plaits and knots, key-pattern and the 'Late-Celtic', the beasts and birds, saints and angels, and all the wealth of varied ornament found in the Lindisfarne Gospels. It means that his design was not based on MS. illumination nor anything but a simple and definite group of requirements, and that he was not Celtic. Nor was he Italian, or he would have drawn his vine leaves. Nor was he Syrian, for one of his rules of composition was to 'keep the eye off the edge', as the old landscape painters'

FIGURE 39. ACCA CROSS, LOWER PART.

precept bade. In the single scrolls of the narrower sides he did it by continual crossing and recrossing of the main stems; on the double scrolls of the broader side he did it by doubling and interweaving the main stems, entirely unlike the hard continuous lines which characterize the treatment of similar motives in the East.

As we go forward we shall see more clearly the reasons for which we consider this Acca cross to be the first great effort in a new kind of art. The rhythm of progress in all such movements has been — first, the effort of a man of genius, creating a design both naturalistic and well thought out; next, the imitations of work that has succeeded, less interesting because made by less competent designers, who nevertheless fancied that

31

they were improving on their model and doing with greater ease and mastery what had been done before with cost and pains,* and thirdly, when the changes have been rung on the theme, a new combination, absorbing the lessons of the past but with fresh motives superadded, by another man of talent or genius who founds a new movement.

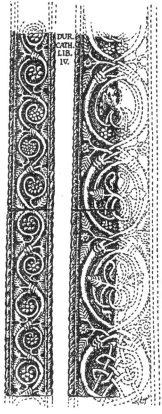

In this process, technical ability grows, effect becomes more of an object, the adaptation of means to end is more considered. There is some gain, and the course of history is not a downward path all the way, for we get such surprises as the Gosforth cross, most beautiful in proportions and effect, with the clumsiest of debased detail. But the path is by no means continuously upward; it is a fallacy to suppose that a 'good' work of art must needs be later than one that seems rude and uncouth, for it is in the nature of things that the first attempt should be finer than those that followed, when it is a question of artistic and not merely workmanlike qualities.

The cross at the foot of Acca's grave is very probably represented by the fragment No. iv at the Cathedral Library, Durham (Fig. 40). When the twelfth century writer saw it, 400 years after the burial of the bishop, and at a time when memorials of this kind had quite gone out of fashion, it may have been believed to represent Acca in some way; but it was not usual to put a tall cross at the grave-foot.† It was, however, usual to ask for a grave as near as possible to the resting-place of some famous saint; and no doubt this cross stood at the head of the *next* grave. Enough of this stone is left to show that it was even thicker in the shaft than Acca's, perhaps bigger in every way, and the design is obviously of the same school. It has the same sort of single and double scrolls, but with differences. The grape-bunches are no longer naturalistic, but have become the berry-bunches, hardly distinguishable from flowers, which we meet often again in later Anglian crosses.

FIGURE 40

* 'We paint,' Vasari said, 'six pictures in a year, while the earlier masters took six years to one picture; and yet these pictures are much more perfectly executed than those of the early school by the most distinguished masters.'

† At a later period small slabs were set up both at the head and the foot of a grave; but crosses truly in pairs are an illusion. See later on Penrith Giant's Grave (Figs. 119,120).

The leaves take a larger place, but they are not vine-leaves; one might suspect them of being rowan-leaves with their berries, except that the rowan-tree was sacred among the pagans and not likely to be acceptable in Christian art. The stems are thickened towards the points where they branch apart, a trick not unknown in Roman Empire design; and they have the branch-bindings characteristic of Anglian scrolls. This cross is therefore not a copy in any sense of Acca's, though it has the same general form of interwoven double-scroll. The cable-edging is conceived as made of two strands, a thick and a thin, wound together; in the Dewsbury 'Paulinus' cross the cable is still further elaborated, and that cross we shall have to place in the ninth century on various grounds, so that this cable is probably later than the simple twist used on Acca's cross. All these indications suggest that in this Durham No. IV we have a distinctly later work, not a previous effort, tentatively leading up to it.

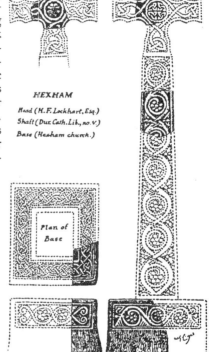

HEXHAM

Head (H.F. Lockhart, Esq.)
Shaft (Dux Cath. Lib., no. V.)
Base (Hexham church.)

Plan of Base

STAMFORDHAM

FIGURE 41   FIGURE 42

Durham No. XII is a fragment from Stamfordham (Fig. 41). The third side is so battered that the attempt to draw it is given with some hesitation, but the rest shows the Hexham motives with real grape-bunches, leaves quite conventional and thickened stems; it is intermediate between the two we have just described.

The shaft (Fig. 37) at the Spital, near Hexham, is closely like the last on three sides (the other narrow side is practically the same as its reverse) and must be of the same

· 33

time, that is to say a little past the middle of the eighth century. But it has on the front the Crucifixion, which may have been suggested by the Hexham Rood-figure.

There is only one other cross attributable to Hexham by its provenance, and that is the monument we venture to put together (Fig. 42) from three fragments, now dispersed, but all from the church. Here one sees an obviously late survival of the double-scroll with leaves conventionalized into stiffness. The head has in its centre the four *triquetrae* we have seen on an Irish slab of 994; not that this need be so late by far, but indicating that the type as a whole is not early. The base has a stiff-leaved scroll and an ingenious plait, but not the kind of plait we shall find in the Anglo-Danish period. This is therefore pre-Danish but late Anglian—that is, about the middle of the ninth century.

The Hexham double scroll travelled in various directions, or at least we

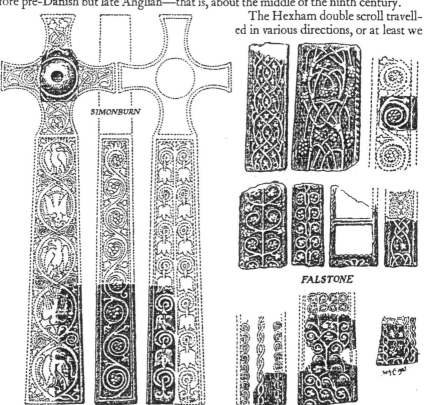

SIMONBURN

FALSTONE

FIGURE 43

FIGURE 44

34

can say that the pattern used on Acca's cross, and those derived from it, reappear elsewhere over a considerable area. The cross suggested by two fragments at Simonburn (Fig. 43) had upon one side a panel repeating the motive, though with details elaborated. At Falstone up the North Tyne valley, one of the stones (Fig. 44) shows a rather late treatment of the same idea in association with fragments of tree-scrolls and some unusual patterns which seem to be of the Anglian survival in this non-Danish area. They are

FIGURE 45

all perhaps by the same hand, the hand of a designer of pleasant fancy though little technical experience; he must have seen Acca's cross and profited by it. And at Nunnykirk, which Mr Cadwallader Bates identified with the Uetadun of Bede, but very long after the days of Bede, a remarkable and skilfully designed cross-shaft (Fig. 45) was made of which one side uses this double scroll combined with birds and beasts. The reverse is ornamented with a pair of single scrolls overlapping and interlocked, neither a double scroll nor a tree scroll; and this, with the offset, is so unusual in pure Anglian work that we must class it by itself, only remarking that the way in which the grape-bunches come almost straight and stiff from

LANCASTER

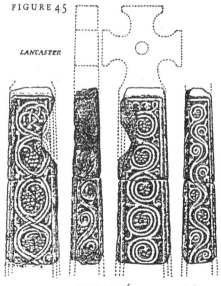

FIGURE 46

35

the volutes of the stalk is less natural than the flowing line of earlier Hexham design. It is a conventionalism in the direction of the second Ilkley cross (Fig. 62) which can hardly be earlier than the middle of the ninth century. Much however of the naturalism and flow of the best Hexham work is preserved in the Nunnykirk stone, and if it is not eighth century and of the best period no more is it tenth century and of the Anglian decadence.

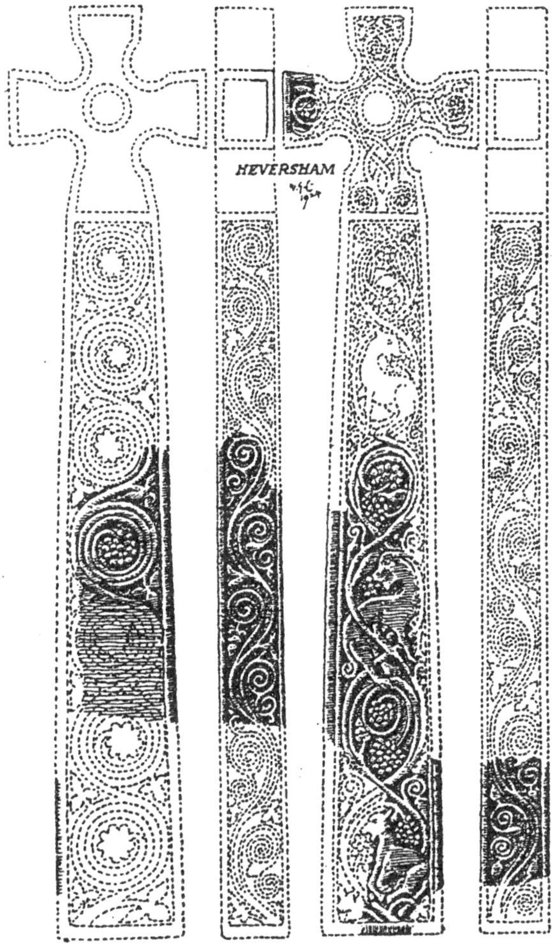

Turning towards the south-west, we find at Lancaster a close reproduction, coarsened a little, of the Acca type (Fig. 46). At that place one is tempted to believe that there was a considerable Anglian abbey, though no records of such a foundation exist beyond the many fragments of monuments discovered in the fabric of the church. What is more, the distinct influence of Lancaster as an Anglian centre is shown in a group of outlying cross-sites—at Halton, Heysham, Heversham and perhaps Kendal, Urswick, and as far as Waberthwaite on the west coast of Cumberland. Fig. 46 at Lancaster, likely to be the earliest there, shows its Hexham origin; the shaft has nothing but single and double scrolls. The piece now at Kendal church may possibly have been taken from Lancaster; its provenance is not certain; but it shows pattern of the same character though with the stiff-set

HEVERSHAM

FIGURE 47

leaf as at Nunnykirk, arguing the later Anglian period. At Kendal there must have been a pre-Norman church; the name of the place was 'Kircabi in Kendale' before 1100; though we do not know that there was a church in pre-Danish days. Lancaster and its

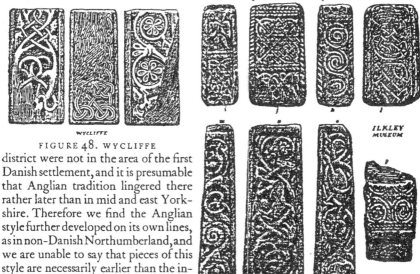

FIGURE 48. WYCLIFFE

FIGURE 49

district were not in the area of the first Danish settlement, and it is presumable that Anglian tradition lingered there rather later than in mid and east Yorkshire. Therefore we find the Anglian style further developed on its own lines, as in non-Danish Northumberland, and we are unable to say that pieces of this style are necessarily earlier than the invasion. But it is probable that this very fair imitation of the Acca patterns is not much, if at all, later than 800, and that Lancaster, in its earlier days, was in close touch with Hexham.

Within an easy day's ride is Heversham, where the fragment of shaft and one of cross-head suggest the restoration of a very interesting monument, in which a late reflection of the Hexham type is seen (Fig. 47). The church there was anciently St Peter's, an Anglian dedication. In the 'Historia de S. Cuthberto' mention is made of an abbot Tilred of 'Hefresham' about 920, which cannot mean Evesham because there is no abbot of that name (see Dugdale's list) to fit the statement. Tilred left Heversham to become ultimately abbot of Norham in Northumberland, no doubt forsaking his first abbey at the time (c. 920) when the Norse settlers arrived in the neighbourhood. This suggests a limit for the date of the cross; it is late Anglian, but not later than the Norse arrival, and the decadence in style shown by it means that it must be nearly as late as that would imply.

Starting again from Hexham southward to Yorkshire, we find at Wycliffe on the Tees a piece (Fig. 48) reminiscent of the style. One side of the great cross (Fig. 52)

37

at Otley (perhaps seen more easily in my reconstruction now in the churchyard as a war-memorial than in the fragments at the church) has a bold double-scroll pattern based on the Acca type though considerably modified. At Dewsbury, one panel (Fig. 91) of the 'Paulinus' cross is filled with a rather debased ninth century double scroll. At Ilkley in the Museum is a fragment (Fig. 49) with a fox eating grapes in a double scroll of decadent character. And finally at the Museum in Hull there is part of a cross-shaft from Patrington in Holderness, showing a motive derived from this Hexham type, also of late Anglian but apparently pre-Danish date.

In this list are included only the examples of double scrolls, for the single scroll is not so distinctive of Hexham influence. Its developments, which might have come from other sources, are considered in the next chapter. But as to the general provenance of the scroll and its use on crosses we must remember that such ornament was common property of all Christendom, derived no doubt from the Constantinian vine, as an emblem usually meant to refer to the Gospel text, 'I am the Vine and ye are the branches.' It was a confession of faith and a statement of Christian hope, most suitable for a place on a grave-monument—the epitaph of any believer. The object in putting it on a cross was not merely decorative. If mere decoration had been intended, there were many kinds of ornament known in the seventh and eighth centuries which would have served as well. But starting with this intention of symbolism, the cross-carvers kept to their own lines. They did not look into illuminated manuscripts and pick out bits of pattern to work into their designs; in all probability the carvers, who for anything we can learn were not monks and clerks but 'smiths', never looked at books at all. They carried on their rough and dirty business in the open, or in the shed of the mason's yard; writers and minature painters worked in a very different way indoors and were quite another class of craftsmen. Therefore we can conceive the two arts as distinct, having their own separate rules and developing on their own separate lines. And even if we knew for a certainty the dates of the various MSS. they would help us little in the study of the crosses; they only illustrate the general and widespread diffusion of a number of forms of art characteristic of the age. As we had to take the crossed slabs on their own terms so we must follow out the sequence of the tall crosses as best we can without importing side-issues and extraneous complications.

Chapter VI. The Tree of Life

WE have just seen that the first intention of grave-monuments was symbolism, and not mere decoration. But by the eighth century that symbolism had taken various shapes. Already the vine had become the 'Tree of Life and a purely Christian emblem had been grafted upon Hellenistic ideas and Roman embellishments such as we see in the Ara Pacis Augustae. Indeed, the development would be natural, even to a hermit. He had heard, 'Unto what is the Kingdom of God like? It is like a grain of mustardseed which a man took and cast into his garden; and it grew, and waxed a great tree; and the fowls of the air lodged in the branches of it.' And again in the psalm *Benedic anima mea*, 'The trees of the Lord are full of sap ... Wherein the birds make their nests ... The high hills are a refuge for the wild goats and so are the strong rocks for the conies.' All over Christendom the populated Tree of Life was familiar; no more is needed to suggest the bird and beast scrolls as an alternative to the Acca vine.

If we can place the examples of this Anglian motive in anything like a series, they will explain themselves. Their original home in Northumbria was not Hexham; we must look for it elsewhere. A likely region is the area influenced by the sister houses of Monkwearmouth and Jarrow. But at these sites we search in vain. It is true that there are pieces at Jarrow—the two birds and the huntsman—of this type; but by their style and cutting they rank later than the beginnings; they are rather of the school which produced the Rothbury cross at a late Anglian period. The Monkwearmouth beasts, in the string-course and on panels, are certainly not Benedict Biscop's work, but of the eleventh century restoration, coeval with Eilaf's at Hexham. We have mentioned the Ormside Cup, and in it we see the birds in the boughs; but though it illustrates current ideas it does not give us a starting-point for the series in stone.

Because it is geographically nearest to the primitive centre, let us take first St Andrew's, Auckland, where are the remains of a fine cross-shaft (Fig. 50) with a great base which seems to have supported it. The saints and angels are far from conventional; they are, if anything, only too naturalistic, the attempt of a carver inexperienced in figure sculpture to make what he thought portraits and to realize details for which the low relief left him too little scope. All Anglian carving suffers in the same way; the ground is sunk deep, and the whole figure brought up nearly to one plane, so that when it comes to shaping the features of the face and the hands there is nothing for it but to suggest them with incised lines. This Auckland carver had never looked at classic work to learn what modelling means; he had no idea of the come-and-go of surface; but he did his best to make PA[VLV]S venerable and AND[REAS] benign, and his sense of proportion is a very great improvement on the disproportioned dwarfs of St Cuthbert's coffin. His birds and beasts are much more skilfully drawn; they are delicately detailed and painstakingly naturalistic. They have not learnt to stand on the boughs, as they do

FIGURE 50

later, but they are alive. For which reason we find this cross a rather early place in the series; indeed, there is nothing that has so many tokens of nascent art. If it is not so successful technically as Acca's, it is because the carver attempted difficulties which the Hexham man wisely avoided. It must be later than the coffin; well on into the eighth century, and the product of a school alien to Hexham and trying to outdo Hexham by breaking fresh ground. But it can hardly be so late as the main group of Anglian crosses, for by their time conventions had been adopted which would have simplified the design and made the work easier.

It is curious that nothing follows very closely after this example. We find next a

FIGURE 51

group with a good deal of similarity, all seeming to belong to the fully developed art. We have of course Ruthwell and Bewcastle—fine but by no means severe or early specimens of the motive. Between the two places is Hoddam, where it seems that an Anglian abbey must have existed from quite ancient times, although there is no mention of it in writing, unless the Tigbrethingham of Symeon's 'Recapitulatio' can be identi-

40

fied with it. But beside the piece from Hoddam at Edinburgh with much likeness to that at Heysham, in which figures are seen at doors and windows of a building (Figs. 88, 89) the fragments from Knockhill seem to be capable of restoration into several handsome crosses. The illustration (Fig. 51) gives two, with spatulated cross-arms and a seated Christ (Majestas) in the centre of the head. The ornament of these appears to be com-

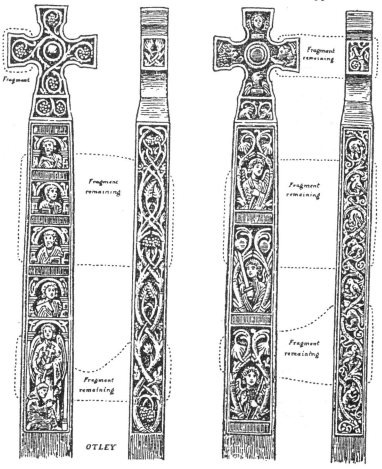

FIGURE 52

posed of small figures, half-length, and little beasts in scroll-work. What the shafts bore is at present unknown; the cross which is drawn between them is evidently of a later date, for its loose scroll is like the later Anglian of the Lancaster school. Perhaps we may assign these of Hoddam to shortly after 800; the Lamb cross between them may be somewhat later.

The 'Angel' cross at Otley, restored from fragments (Fig. 52) must have been one of the very finest in artistic attainment. A fragment of vine-scroll gives the head. On one side, busts of the four evangelists (three exist), with their books as on St Cuthbert's coffin, appear under arches. Below can be traced an angel; one wing, some fine drapery and the butt-end of the cross he is holding are plain to see; with the charmingly carved head of a monk (as he seems to be by his cowl) kneeling at the angel's feet. This is a motive found again in the 'Paulinus' cross at Dewsbury and in another at Halton church near Lancaster, showing that it was an accepted idea. On a grave-stone it must intend resignation and hope, poetically symbolized. The reverse of this shaft has given some trouble to follow out in its details. At first it seemed that the great pairs of boughs with their big leaves and fruit were meant to be filled with leaf-forms or, perhaps, in the case of the uppermost one, with a winged dragon; but further close study has shown that the lowest arch certainly contained a curly head, and the uppermost had the much-battered figure of an angel with wings. In the restoration therefore they are boldly supplied and it is suggested that they represent Michael, Raphael and Gabriel. The fourth side with its reminiscence of the Hexham double scroll has already been mentioned; and the remaining edge has a well-drawn and cleverly carved bird-and-beast scroll. The date of this cannot be far away from that of similar work at Hoddam.

Easby church in N.W. Yorkshire must have been Anglian long before it was restored in the twelfth century and the Premonstratensian house founded (1151-2) near it. Into the fabric are built two fragments of a cross-shaft, and another in the possession of Mr Jaques gives the suggestion of a very fine cross (Fig. 53). The Majestas, much weathered, is a good example of the higher reach of Anglian figure-sculpture, and on the reverse is a complicated scroll with an elaborately detailed eagle and one of nondescript though prettily drawn beasts of this central period of Anglian art. As to the date, if the built-in stones are part of the same cross, we get some hint in the closed figures-of-eight in the plait. Such closed forms become more and more common as time goes on; they occur at Thornhill (Yorks.) in work not before the middle of the ninth century, but they do not occur in stones we can date early, though possibly in MS. ornament. It must surely be inferred from this plait and the florid scroll and the ambitious figure-carving that Easby cross was not one of the earliest, but that the school was at its meridian when this was produced.

At Hovingham (west of Malton, Yorks.) is a slab (Fig. 54) which seems to be not of a monument but something like a reredos or screen, and to date from about this period. The horizontal course of scroll-work at the foot, with birds and beasts of the same Anglian style, has the branch-bindings at the joints of the boughs which are usual in pre-Norman work, but not later. The arched panels, each filled with a nimbed figure, resemble in a general way those of the monument at Peterborough, formerly attributed to Abbot Hedda (died 870) but of the tenth century as shown by the animal-scrolls. The figures at Hovingham are much more graceful, more Anglian and early in design; the first two panels, representing the Annunciation, are indeed so charming that doubt has been very naturally thrown on their pre-Norman date. Taken however with other examples of the series it does not seem impossible; on the contrary, a later age which produced the grotesque hogback figured with this slab was quite unable to conceive anything so dainty.

EASBY

The Masham shaft we have already noticed for its general shape; here we have to mention it for the row of animals in the lowest tier (Fig. 55). The stone is so weathered that details cannot be made out; the head and the horns(?) of the last of the row are now a group of corroded holes; but the stag in the middle is fairly plain and the giraffe-like creatures we see again at Crofton. All have the same feeling for design which must have been general in this central Anglian period and entirely different from any Anglo-Danish or Norman work.

FIGURE 53

At West Tanfield, a short distance S.E. of Masham, is a shaft-fragment (Fig. 56) with more beasts of the same kind and no doubt of the same date.

Another very accomplished piece of this kind is the slab at Jedburgh (Fig. 57). The carving of the birds and beasts is as good as it can be, and very perfectly preserved. As a frame to the panel there is a

HOVINGHAM

HELMSLEY

FIGURE 54

43

MASHAM shaft, upper half

MASHAM shaft, lower half

FIGURE 55

plait, and the knots of this plait by comparison with others indicate the ninth century, because they are not seen in any stone that can be dated earlier, but become more common in the later period. Now Symeon of Durham's 'Recapitulatio' (p. 68 of the Surtees Society's volume 51) says that bishop Ecgred founded (*condidit*) the two houses of 'Geddewrd', and he was made bishop in 830. It is possible that there was an abbey or a church there before that, but the statement suggests, what is likely upon typological grounds, that the stone cannot be earlier than the second quarter of the ninth century.

The Jedburgh details show that we have come to a time when the followers of the best designers began to forsake their ideals. They drew their beasts a little more grotesque, feeling perhaps, as the diadochi of other schools have felt, that prettiness was out of date, and piquancy more in demand. To this stage belongs the highly interesting shaft at Cundall (Fig. 32) with late Anglian (but not Celtic) plaits and a new taste in the disposition of its panels. The Rev. H. Stapleton of Kirby Hill suggests that the stone possibly represents one of

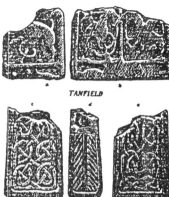

TANFIELD

FIGURE 56

three crosses noticed by Leland (temp. Henry VIII) on the site of the old Ripon monastery, and that it may have been taken to Cundall to be used as a lintel, for so it is represented in Whitaker's plate (Richmond, ii, 195). In 1915 Mr George W. Haswell, F.S.A., of Chester suggested the restoration with stones then at the Aldborough museum, and in 1918 it was proposed to reunite the fragments and to restore the whole to Cundall. Whether the figures at the foot represent the Raising of Lazarus and what stood in the arch above them is uncertain; but the arches are interesting for their impost-capitals, the Ravenna type of 'pulvin' (Rivoira, 'Lomb. Arch.' i, 85, etc.) and finely illustrated in Giacomo Boni's paper on Parenzo ('Archivio Storico dell'Arte', 1894) long antecedent to the period of this stone.

JEDBURGH

FIGURE 57

45

And though some of the beasts are almost as pretty as ever, others are distinctly grotesque. One is particularly worth mention—straining his neck down between his forelegs to get at the berry-bunch near the root of the tree. We have met that creature again (pp. 24, 25 and see p. 51).

Not unlike the Cundall animals are those on the recumbent monument at Melsonby (Fig. 20); they are still Anglian but losing their charm and becoming more clumsy.

FIGURE 58

The pair in the middle seem at first sight to have lost their heads; in reality the heads have been drawn like that of the uppermost beast on the second side at Cundall—not in profile but as if looked down upon. This was no doubt intended to vary the old and easy trick of outlining a head in profile, which nevertheless is much more suited to relief-carving of this elementary sort. The scroll adjacent is thickened and stiffened from the earlier style; the plait on the other side is a late though pre-Danish Anglian motive, not found in Celtic monuments. And the rows of heads looking out of portholes on the side of the monument remind one of the 'dolls' house' design of Hoddam and Heysham; it is certainly ninth century. The carving is very clever and crisp: in the sister stone some of the work is even undercut, showing that technique had advanced *pari passu* with the process that made design florid.

Another example of this class is the fragment of a cross-shaft found about 1910 at Dacre, Cumberland, now in the church there (Fig. 58). The arris splits as it descends so that it must have been one of the round-shafted type and like the Collingham 'Apos-

46

tles' cross. It is extremely clever in its chisel-work; the details are minutely wrought out, as for example the military-looking lion's face and the little feet above that. But the flat-strap scroll runs into key-pattern, and this means the later part of the Anglian, pre-Danish period. It would be especially interesting if we could date it, because Bede mentions the abbey 'by the river of Dacore' as the scene of a cure by means of a relic of St Cuthbert and gives the names of two abbots, Swithbert and Thridred. The other

CROFT

FIGURE 59

cross at Dacre is certainly much later, but this one, by comparison in the series, may be placed perhaps not more than a hundred years after Bede, and its presence adds very greatly to the identification of the site as one famous in history.

Similar in delicate carving is the piece of a small and dainty cross at Croft, near Darlington (Fig. 59). Its beasts and birds are highly stylized; they are by no means early in this series. The tree-scroll usually goes with rather later work than the simple alternating volutes. The plait is one seen only in late Anglian examples, such as Thornhill and Closeburn (Dumfriesshire) and the stone we have next to examine.

At Otley there was a second cross of some importance (Fig. 60) besides many smaller monuments. On the shaft are saints of which one is carved in high relief as on the 'Angel' cross, and the other sketched with incised lines, whether unfinished or meant to be left so and painted up into effect we can hardly say. Above a step is a narrower neck of shaft connecting with the head, of which there is a little part remaining, and this part shows rather late drapery, as if angels or other figures had a place on the cross-head. Two sides of the narrowing shaft bear dragons, very cleanly and neatly chiselled with more roundness than usual in Anglian relief; they must be of this period of advanced technique. On one of the narrower faces are two beasts, one upside-down, their tails tied together in a Carrick bend: this treatment of beasts we have not seen before

47

except at Croft, but we find it often again and it is a late motive frequent in the tenth century. Finally the plait is as on the Croft stone but in flat and shallow cutting and with angularities that suggest later date because early interlacing is in flowing curves, gradually becoming more and more angular until in the eleventh century it is sometimes merely a tangle of zig-zag. All combines to give this cross a date approaching the middle of the ninth century.

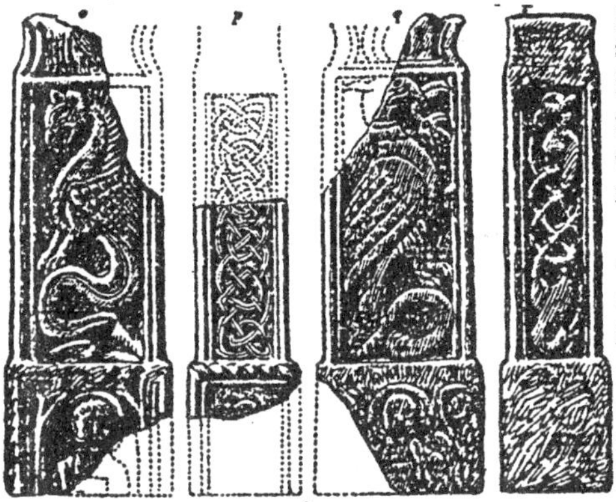

At Ilkley church there are three well-known crosses; on the tallest (Fig. 63) was affixed in 1914 a head from Middleton Hall but originally no doubt from this church. It may not be the head of that shaft, but that shaft offered the most convenient place for its preservation and display, and it is of the same general character and style.

Of the three the shortest (Fig. 61) is obviously cut down. It bears a much weathered saint with his book; above him a band of plait seen at Melsonby and Dewsbury and on tenth century stones at Otley and Kildwick-in-Craven. This meant that the shaft is not an early attempt and though the beasts still have some of the old swing in their lines, not only are they on the way to losing it and becoming grotesque but the plaits in which they are entangled are not leaf-scrolls but straps such as we see commonly in the Viking Age. The

FIGURE 60. OTLEY

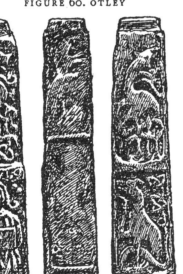

i   j   *ILKLEY CH.*   k   l

FIGURE 61

48

animal with long horns, or perhaps ears, and kicking up a hind leg, we have not seen before on crosses; but it must have meant something, for it appears on a coin of Eadberht (737-758) a century earlier than this cross is likely to be.

The second cross at Ilkley church (Fig. 62) has the sharp carving of the Otley dragons though very differently designed. The scrolls have the stiff-set leaf which we have noticed as a late trick; it is part of the attempt to get more piquancy into the pattern. The animals are still more grotesque, and yet one can see that they are from the same source. The creature in the lower panel of the third side is another example of the head seen from above, not in profile. The birds had morsels of lead let into their eyes, perhaps a setting for jewels: for there can be no doubt that the crosses were usually polychromatic — traces of paint are found on some — and in later stones there are often holes in the centres of the crossheads in which bits of bright glass must have been set like the jewels of the Ormside cup. By its comparatively debased design, this second Ilkley cross may be rather later than others of the cleverly carved group; perhaps about the middle of the ninth century.

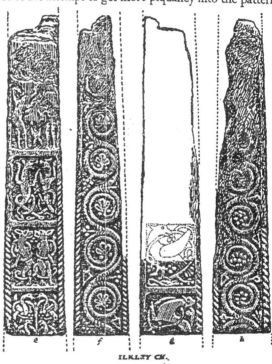

ILKLEY CH.

FIGURE 62

The tallest of the three (Fig. 63) seems to be later still. The scrolls of the narrower sides are now varied — a sign of the attempt of decadence to be picturesque. Unnecessary *triquetrae* fill a couple of spandrils, but otherwise there is no interlacing. The four evangelists with their symbolic heads may be described as a triumph of bold design in flat relief; they are decorative and 'carry' like a good poster. The Majestas at the top of the other side shows the limitations of the late period; figure-carving to suggest relief was too much for the workman. And the animals below, bold as they are, have lost

49

all the charm and nobility of the fine style. We must place this at the end of the Anglian period proper; it shows no sign of Danish influence and cannot be after the time when the Danes began to alter the taste of the public for whom crosses were set up.

ILKLEY

But the shaft remains unbroken, for in all probability the Danes did not reach Ilkley in their first destructive invasion. The archbishop's refuge was not farther up Wharfedale than the next village; at Addingham he seems to have remained in peace while the invaders overran the flat country and destroyed the churches from Doncaster to Hexham, and Ilkley no doubt shared his immunity. But so important a monument could hardly have been carved in the troublous days of invasion. It must be of the years immediately before 867, when there was still no cloud on the horizon— only the twilight of decadence.

One step more brings us into the moonlight. In the runic shaft (Fig. 31) at Collingham, half way between Ilkley and York, we find the transition from Anglian to Anglo-Danish design, and the beginnings of a new series of monuments, carved under altered influences. On this cross the inscription was formerly thought to refer to King Oswine, whose pathetic story is told by Bede (*Hist.Eccl.*iii,14) —how he was king of Deira and a young man of

FIGURE 63

saintly character, killed in 642 through the jealousy and treachery of King Oswiu of Bernicia. On this misreading and consequent misdating, theories were built up which obscured not only the history of this one monument but of the whole series; for if this cross could be placed in the middle of the seventh century any rational conception of the sequence of Northumbrian crosses is impossible. The runes, however, do not spell 'Oswine' but 'Ærswith[-]'; Dr Wilhelm Vietor read 'Ærswith[un]' followed by R or B ('Die Northumbrischen Runensteine') which does not now seem to be plain. The name is certainly Anglian, and the ultimate origin of the design is from Anglian tradition; but the forms are altered in the direction leading towards tenth century art. On the second side we have the double outline and the joint-spirals of beasts unknown in earlier Anglian art but coming into use late in the ninth century. The plaits in which

they are entangled are no longer vine-tendrils but flat straps, not thrown about at random as in the tenth century but losing much of their regularity; and yet on the first side there is an Anglian scroll and on the fourth a panel of symmetrical knotwork. The animal with its head between its forepaws we have seen before on the Cundall shaft (Fig. 32). The beast with the wrinkled snout appears on the shortest cross (Fig. 61) at Ilkley. Everything points to the persistence of Anglian tradition, but under new conditions of taste, possibly, as we shall see on closer examination (Chapter XIII) of Celtic origin and pre-Danish. But however this may turn out it is obvious that after the Danish settlement

CROFTON

FIGURE 64

of 875 some such change must have occurred. They did not import their own stone-carvers; it is unlikely that they had any; but they imported fresh ideas of treatment and an altered standard of style which was generally accepted.

It may be thought that the acceptance was entirely general and that it was not so much the influence of Danish settlers that created the change as a universal, secular movement, altering taste merely because the older fashions were by that time outworn. That was no doubt the case, in the sense that fine style had disappeared from Anglian art, and some new motives were already creeping in. But that the new taste was especially Danish is probable because it is seen in the neighbourhood of the new-comers' settlements more markedly than in those districts where they did not settle. We have already alluded to the non-Danish areas as showing traces of Anglian survival and further development or decay on Anglian lines; and to anticipate Chapter XIII we may note that (although as the tenth century advanced the Danelaw included northern England in general) for about half a century after the invasion the actual Danish area north of the Humber seems to have been limited to the great central vale of York, the East

51

Riding and County Durham. North of the Tyne, though Halfdan raided and destroyed, there was no regular settlement; the country remained under Anglian lords, and Danish place-names are few. Cleveland, a rough country of hills and dales, does not seem to have attracted the Danes; all indications suggest that it was filled up later by Norse settlers. The western dales of Yorkshire, as we have seen from the fact of archbishop Wulthere's refuge, were also non-Danish, at first, for the same reason. Still more so was all the west country and the land beyond the Solway. Now in these parts we can point to monuments which seem to show the late survival of the Anglian style beyond the stage at which it stops and is transformed at Ilkley and Collingham.

North   West

South   WALTON CROSS   East

FIGURE 65

There is perhaps something not far from true in the statement of the eleventh century Life of St Cadroë (Skene's 'Chronicles of the Picts and Scots', p. 116) that at a date nearing 950 Leeds was the border town between Cumbria and the Northmen. At any rate the old forest of Elmet, west of the line from Leeds to Doncaster, is comparatively free of Danish monuments and place-names, while retaining many late Anglian relics. At Crofton, outside the Danish frontier as Collingham was, we find a piece (Fig. 64) with its distinctly Anglian beasts double-outlined. The cross-head, with a bishop on it, may or may not belong to the shaft: this figure upside down—is it elucidated by the crucifixion of St Peter (Fig. 97)? But nothing could show more plainly that the art of the place was Anglian, though past the Anglian prime and touched, as at Collingham, with newfangled fashions.

At Walton, between Dewsbury and Halifax, there is a great cross-base (Fig. 65)

52

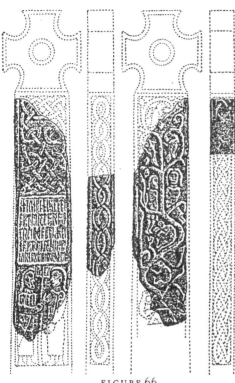

FIGURE 66

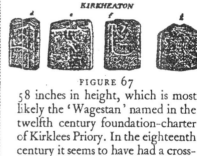

KIRKHEATON

FIGURE 67

58 inches in height, which is most likely the 'Wagestan' named in the twelfth century foundation-charter of Kirklees Priory. In the eighteenth century it seems to have had a cross-shaft standing in the socket-hole, and it must have been an ambitious monument, but not commemorating a pre-Danish personage or a Dane. The plaits are all tenth or even eleventh century in character; the big roundel is unique, but its manner of construction is seen on no stone of early Anglian kind, and the elaborated *triquetrae* are also very late. But the beasts on that side and the birds on the reverse are simply the old Anglian animals debased. At the time, Danish style was prevalent in Danish districts, but this means a survival of the old population in the heart of Elmet; just as the name 'Wala-tūn' implies that when the Angles came they had found the still older 'Welsh' inhabiting this out-of-the-way spot. West Riding wealth did not begin until, in the later middle ages, its water-power invited the erection of fulling-mills and the growth of the woollen industry.

North-west of this we have already noticed Heversham as an Anglian survival into the tenth century. To a not much earlier date we must assign the curious shaft found in 1911 at Urswick in Furness (Fig. 66). That it is uglier and further away from Anglian ideals than the Heversham cross means probably the want of a better craftsman, for the indications do not place it much later; its runes, names, plaits (the double twist of the second side is on a ninth century stone at Leeds), and even the figures, birds and beasts of its crazy scroll are all Anglian and not of the Norse who came to settle in Furness about 920. Its inscription says 'Tunwini set after Torhtred a monument to his lord. Pray for his soul'; and cut across the clumsy saints below is 'Lyl this w[rought]'. True it is that the worse the artist the bolder his signature. An even more debased bit of work at Kirkheaton in Elmet (Fig. 67) is inscribed in Anglian runes 'Eoh wrought [this]' and was unashamed.

In non-Danish Northumberland we have noticed Falstone and the balusters of Simonburn. The attempt (Fig. 43) at a restoration of the Simonburn cross from the centre of the head and a large piece of the shaft at the church shows one of these late Anglian works. The scroll of the edge with stiff-set leaves we have seen at Ilkley and placed at the middle of the ninth century. The tree-scroll of the last side with big bell-flowers is of a later character and the Hexham double scroll with birds alternately standing and hovering is obviously decadent though it need not be very late, for a good deal of Anglian feeling remains in it.

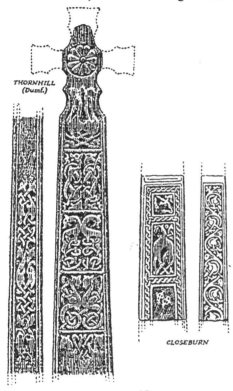

THORNHILL (Dumf.)

CLOSEBURN

FIGURE 68

But in Dumfriesshire that was, with Northumberland, within the ancient diocese of Lindisfarne, there are survivals of the same style carried further. Near Thornhill, beside the road west of the bridge over the Nith, is a cross (Fig. 68) well preserved and pleasant to behold in its native surroundings. It bears a very late kind of plait; any such composite pattern must be of the time when variegated picturesqueness was a studied object; but it has an Anglian free-armed head, not the wheel-cross of the Viking Age. The beasts are not unlike their brothers at Ilkley, clearly Anglian before the flow of

54

line was lost. And in the Grierson Museum at Thornhill is a shaft from Closeburn (Fig. 68) of similar character but in further decadence. In this the bird-scroll looks like an attempt to reproduce the Ruthwell motive; the plait is the plait of Croft and the Otley dragon; but the grotesque little beast that is trying to hold its own feet and the clumsy horse(?) beneath it rank with what we might imagine possible to a generation following the Cundall carver.

These two are hardly of the ninth century, but survivals of the style into the tenth; and one step further—the slab of Wamphray in Dumfriesshire (Fig. 69)—brings us into the Norse period. On the same stone we have a Scandinavian dragon along with leaf-scrolls of Anglian derivation set in the form of the *swastika* imported by the Norse. In this the overlap to Anglo-Norse is as plain as the designer could make it. (For the Norse in that district see Trans. Dumf. and Galloway Ant. Soc. ser. 3, vii, 97 ff.)

We propose taking up the sequel of these two developments—Anglo-Danish and Anglo-Norse—later on; in the meantime we have to go back and retrace the progress of Anglian art by its plaits and by its figure-subjects. We shall find that they tell the same story.

FIGURE 69

Chapter VII. Plaits and Inscriptions.

REFERENCE has been made so often already to plaits or knots of cord or strap interlaced, without leaf-boughs, that we ought not to put off the consideration of this form of ornament too long. In the illustrations we have given so far, it must have been noticed that the finer sort of Anglian crosses, where they have knot-work at all, show symmetrical and ingenious design, while the plaits on Anglo-Danish work tend to greater simplicity and are much less interesting. This is easy to understand on the principle that the earlier carvers took more trouble over their details and the later carvers tried rather for effect, got as cheaply as possible. But the principle requires many limitations and modifications before it can become the expression of the actual process, in various districts; and we must follow out the changes historically, so far as we are able.

The late Mr Romilly Allen, whose work on crosses is invaluable to all students, has given us a complete treatise (in 'Early Christian Monuments of Scotland') on knots and their development *a priori;* but he would have been the last to claim that this represents the facts as they took place in the history of Northumbrian design. It is well-known that in Northumbria we have by no means the beginnings of interlacing, which is an old story in Christian art; unnecessary here to trace back to its origins. But it may be useful to observe contemporary plaits as used in Italy (Fig. 70), remarking that the first is composed of one strap, and drawn in flowing lines; the next differs only in having one member (sketched with a black medial line) closed and separate from the rest. Then follow interlacements more and more broken in effect, more angular and with greater proportion of closed members. This seems to give the normal course of development in the design of interlacing.

We have seen that the Clonmacnois slabs give no examples of plaits until the tenth century; but that slab-design ought to be considered as a separate art, carried on within its own limits, just as manuscript ornament was a separate art exerting little influence on masonry. Neither of these affords conclusive proofs of the age of a stone cross, which must be taken on terms of stone crosses as a series. Not only the design of the Whithorn St Peter's stone has no plaits but the Hex-

Cividale, about 737.

Valpolicella ciborium, 712-740

San Pietro, Toscanella, dated by Rivoira 739; (pattern common in 9th cent.)

Cattaro (Ravenna or Comacine work) 809.

S. Apollinare in Classe, ciborium, 9th cent.

San Flaviano, Montefiascone, 1032.

Sant'Ambrogio, Milan, 11th cent.

FIGURE 70

ham School, which we have dated from 740 onward, and the rival school of animal-scrolls begin their careers without interlaced cords or straps. The leaf-boughs are interwoven, but they are primarily leaf-boughs rather than knots. There are no knots on the Ruthwell cross, but very elaborate and highly developed plaits on the Bewcastle shaft which is in so many ways akin to it. By the time the Bewcastle shaft was designed, interlaced work was not only well understood but had advanced to its highest standard of complication and intellectual effort.

Now, do we begin with high development and gradually degrade? We want some fixed points on which to hang our ladder of examples, and perhaps the following series may provide enough in that way to climb what otherwise seems an inaccessible rock-face. We get a few examples with both inscriptions and plaits; the inscriptions give some hint of the age, not very definite but dividing at any rate Anglian from Anglo-Danish strata; and the knots can be compared with those of other stones, on the princi-

ple that borrowing is more like-ly than inventing. In the nascent stage of art, invention is possible and probable; in the decadence, easy-going re-use of old motives is the rule. But at any time, as we have already observed, some capable, native-born or foreign-instructed craftsman may strike in and upset all our pretty rules. And in fact, to anticipate the result, we may say that it was so. We do find highly ingenious knots along with work we must judge by many concurrent indications to be early; we find

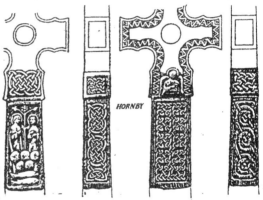

HORNBY

FIGURE 71

cheaply-planned or carelessly drawn knots on late work, especially of the Anglo-Danish school; but at various times and places later, we see the evidence of fresh efforts, issuing in the wonderful elaboration of the Scottish cross-slabs.

One of the most remarkable of Anglian monuments, because of its delicacy and beauty, is the little stone at Hornby church in Lonsdale (Fig. 71) from the walls of a barn at Hornby Priory site. On the shaft is the Miracle of the Loaves and Fishes, very daintily drawn and cut like the work we have attributed at Dacre and elsewhere to the early part of the ninth century. On the reverse is an angel holding a book—perhaps the Book of Remembrance, as at Halton. Under the first panel below the angel is the beginning of an inscription—'[?D]N.dIRI[GE?]'—possibly, but not by any means certainly, the opening of the Dirge or Antiphon in the Office for the Dead; at any rate

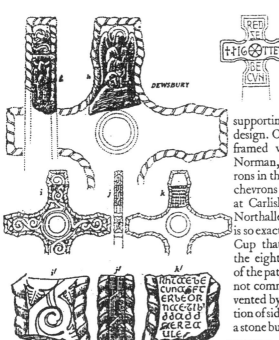

DEWSBURY

FIGURE 73

FIGURE 72

supporting the Anglian character of the design. On that side the head has been framed with chevrons pelleted; not Norman, for we have seen incised chevrons in the earliest Hexham stones, and chevrons in relief occur in Anglian heads at Carlisle and Ripon and on one at Northallerton, of which the ornament is so exactly like the base of the Ormside Cup that it cannot be other than of the eighth or ninth century. The rest of the patterns on the Hornby stone are not common-form but apparently invented by the designer, with the exception of side *d*. This has a plait like one on a stone built into a buttress of Ripon Ca-

thedral, and seen also at Hoddam. Later examples of this plait are at Chester-le-Street and other places, for it became fairly frequent. Taking all together one can hardly doubt that this is a bit of the work of the Ripon school and carved rather early in the ninth century.

At Carlisle, part of a cross-head kept in the Fratry (Fig. 72) has on its arm-ends only a couple of knots, one of them made from two members woven into a Carrick bend. But the inscription is in good Anglian—SIG[RED SE]TTE DIS [BECVN] AEF[TER[SVITBERH[TAE]—'Sigred set this monument after Swithbert'.

58

LANCASTER

FIGURE 74

The form of the D, which is not crossed though aspirated, indicates a period hardly advanced into the ninth century, to judge (as noticed before) from the lettering on coins.

In the British Museum from Dewsbury is part of a cross-head (Fig. 73 *i j k*) delicately carved and bearing in minuscules ... *rhtae becun aefter beornae. gibiddadd der saule:*—'[Someone set this in memory of]—berht, a monument to his lord. Pray for his soul.' The scroll on the reverse has the stiff-set leaf indicating the middle of the ninth century; and the rectangular twist on the edge does not occur in any very early stone-work; it seems to tell us that we are coming towards the time when straight-lined patterns were in favour.

Fragments at Lancaster of a cross which can be restored (Fig. 74) with approximate certainty give the inscription — ✠ ORATE P[RO] ANIMA HARD[VV]INI, together with indications of the regular plait on the head, and scrolls of the type found at Ilkley and elsewhere with the leaf branching stiffly away from the volute. The tendency to vary these scrolls suggests a rather late time in the ninth century, but direct descent from the normal Hexham type of work, although the Hexham double-scroll is not illustrated in this example.

Hackness, near Scarborough, was founded by St Hilda herself in 680 as a cell of Whitby. Bede's story of the nun Begu (*Hist. Eccl.* iv, 23), who has been mistakenly confused by medieval writers with the patroness of St Bees, is located there; but in 869 the house was destroyed by the Danes and not restored until late in the eleventh century. Fragments of an important cross (Fig. 75) remain. The inscriptions are tantalizing. Father Haigh gave a reading ('Yorks. Archaeol. Journ.' vol. iii) which can now be made out only in part, and the historical inferences he drew

FIGURE 75

59

are not convincing. As it stands we read on side *a*— ... GA SEMPER TE [A]MENT MEMORES DOMUS TU[A]E TE MATE[R] AMANTISSIMA —'[O Æthelburga?] may thy houses (i.e. nunneries) ever be mindful of thee and love thee, most

FIGURE 76

loving mother.' And below— ... ✠ SC.E ... S ... ABBADISSA OEDILBURGA ORATE PR[O NOBIS]—'St.—[and?] abbess Æthelburga,* pray ye for us.' On another side (not here drawn)—OEDIL-BURGA BEATA AD SEMPER TE RECOL-ANT AMANTES PIE DEPOSCANT RE-QUIEM SEMPITERNAM SANCTORUM PIA MATER APOSTOLICA, — 'Blessed Æthelburga, may thy lovers ever remember thee: may they dutifully pray for the eternal repose of the saints, kind mother apostolic.' In these phrases we have evidence that the cross was made by or for nuns, and therefore must have been erected before the destruction of the nunnery and not — for example — by King Æthelstan on his northern visit. On the third side there is a mutilated panel of runes (shown enlarged in Fig. 76) — ✠ MMCN[G?]NŒ[S?] / GNWGIH [S?] Œ[B?] followed by four lines of twig-runes which end with ORA ... broken off; and then in another panel below are cryptic figures which hitherto have defied interpretation (Fig. 77). Twig-runes are usually soluble by considering the 'futhorc' or runic alphabet as divided into groups; the number of twigs on the first side of the stem gives the group and those on the other side tell the place of the rune therein. But these forms are much defaced; they do not seem to read now as they appeared to Haigh, who supplied Figure 84 in Huebner's 'Inscriptiones Brit. Christ.' With all that has been done to interpret them we get only another series of isolated letters, not a phrase of words. Haigh thought they might be the initials of those who helped to raise the monument; it seems like a counsel of despair, but we can get no nearer. It would be a kind of *Liber Vitae* of the nunnery.

The question is about the age of the inscriptions. There are twig-runes on the Andreas stone, I. o. Man,

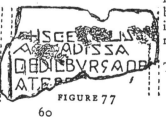

FIGURE 77

60

---

* Several abbesses of the name are recorded but none in close connexion with Whitby.

which Dr Shetelig classes ('Saga-book of the Viking Society', 1925) as of Gaut Bjarnarson's followers, whom he dates about 950-1000; but these are much more advanced in character than the simple fir-trees at Hackness. There is the late Scandinavian short rune for S, somewhat resembling that which may be doubtfully read on the Hackness panel; but the Hackness form is in the lower (not the upper) register and more nearly resembles the form on the Thames knife, rather late Anglian. The rune here read [G?] is like the later H, but we find it on the stone (Fig. 78) at Thornhill (Yorks.) beginning the Anglian name *Gilsuith* and apparently meaning an unvoiced G. The Hackness runes are therefore Anglian but not very early.

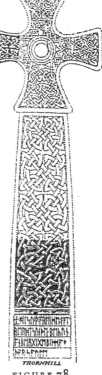

Another indication of lateness is the double outline to the beasts' legs.* We saw it on the Collingham ' Ærswith' stone, but associated with further developments. Here it seems to suggest the beginning of the new style which must have crept in during the ninth century and though it flourished later in a more marked form was perhaps not simply a Danish importation. And finally the plaits. That under the cryptograms is found elsewhere only at Melsonby, on a stone we have placed in the ninth century. The plait above is one that, a little later, is fairly common, but it is unseen earlier. We get a date for the Hackness cross, therefore, not long before 869 and we see that by that time the early complicated knots were being supplanted by simplified motives.

Thornhill (Yorks.) we have just mentioned. It was in the comparatively non-Danish forest of Elmet where Anglian traditions lingered a while. The Osbercht slab (Fig. 23) has been described, and its plait has a resemblance to that of the stone (Fig. 78) inscribed in runes:—*Gilsuith araerde aeft Berhtsuithe becun [on?] bergi. Gebiddath thaer saule;* 'Gilsuith reared [this cross] to Berhtsuith, a monument on her grave. Pray for her soul.' And the plait is rather simply constructed; not used in early crosses, but in later work, especially Scottish, as at Nigg and St Andrew's. It appears therefore first in Northumbria late in the ninth century, if that, as we infer, is the date of these Thornhill stones.

At Durham Cathedral Library (No. 50, figured in the Durham Catalogue), from Yarm near the Tees, is part of a cross-shaft inscribed in minuscules ' . . . [He]riberecht

FIGURE 78

---

* Close inspection seems to show that both the beasts had double outlines. One leg however is partly defaced and it is drawn in Fig. 75 as it appeared to the naked eye.

the priest. Alla set [this] cross (*signum*) after his brother.' The plait beneath is made of the same Stafford-knot as that of Gilsuith's, but differently arranged, and in this form it is very common on late stones, as at Ilkley, and in county Durham and the Midlands, in Scotland and Wales. On the edges of the stone are running patterns of volutes with an almost Celtic aspect, but like those under the Simonburn balusters. On the reverse are two square panels of simple design, not key-pattern but very unlike anything we find on Anglian stones of the earlier period. We must class this as of the Anglian survival on the fringe of the Danish district, and after the restoration of Christianity by King Guthred (880-90). There is plenty of evidence that after this time there was a renaissance in the north of Northumbria, though the excellence of earlier Anglian art was never recaptured.

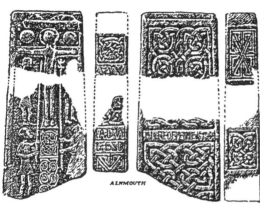

ALNMOUTH

FIGURE 79

Near the ruins of the church at Alnmouth were found in 1789 the fragments (Fig. 79) of a cross-shaft (taken to Alnwick Castle) with '[Pray for the] soul of Eadulf D.' and 'Myredah [made me?]'. The first words are in uncials; the second phrase is in mixed ordinary letters and runes, such a mixture as we see on ninth and tenth century coins of Northumbria, e.g. one of Æthelstan struck at EOFORPIC (York) where P is the rune for W. It is misleading to try, with Father Haigh, a guess at the Eadulf here named, and the lettering is not so early as the date he gave the stone. It bears an interesting Crucifixion with the Spear-bearer and the Sponge-bearer, and two other figures under the cross; but the Christ is not draped in a long garment as in earlier stones. The plaits are fairly complicated, but not made with flowing lines like those of Bewcastle and such other fine works; we see here the beginning of the elaboration of stiff detail which takes so large a place in Scottish slabs. Under the Crucifix and over 'Myredah' is a motive identical with one at Lindisfarne; the square-formed key-pattern is also found at Lindisfarne. The plait under 'Myredah' is not seen elsewhere; the nearest to it is on the Bewcastle cross. And over 'Eadulf' is a pattern like those found at Durham, where historical evidence indicates the end of the tenth century. Some time in that century, but while the old traditions were strong, must be the date of this stone: and we find in it the fruit of the revival of craftsmanship in a northern school, whose work is seen also at Lindisfarne, though the abbey there had been destroyed. As at Hexham, no doubt, the site was still

62

used for burial. We must also remember that the Danes had become decent Christians, on the whole, though the Anglian abbeys had not been reconstructed as such.

The ugly cross at Urswick we have already described (Fig. 66) and dated by what can be gathered of the history of the place to a-bout 900 or a trifle later. Its knots are much debased, with a pretence of symmetry but crudely drawn: on the edge is the double twist seen in a ninth century Ilkley stone and part of

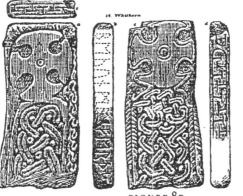

FIGURE 80

a running plait of four, common in the tenth century but not earlier. Its runes, with Anglian, non-Danish names, speak for themselves, and proclaim that a rustic craftsman rather than a very late period was answerable for this abortion.

Another development we must not omit—the transition from Anglian to Cumbrian and thence to Scottish art in the north-west. At Whithorn Museum and at St Ninian's Cave are two crosses (Fig. 80) much alike and both inscribed with Anglian runes. The first has the inscription in bold characters along one edge:—[*Becun Do*]*nferths*, 'the monument of Donferth', the tenth century form of an Anglian name. The other has nothing left but '*wrote*' at the end of a line, from which the rest has been broken off, but the whole was obviously common-form—'✠ So-and-so *wrought* this cross after Someone; pray for his soul'. The date of the disuse of such runes, replaced by Scandinavian, is not easy to fix, but some time in the tenth century they must have died out, though occasional runes survived for ages, as already noted on coins. Indeed, in the vulgar sign of 'Ye olde Bacca Shoppe' we see even nowadays the last remnant of the runic 'thorn' for *th*. But these crosses are certainly not earlier than the tenth century because one of them has the T⊥T pattern which is characteristic of that period; it is found on a late Anglian cross at Kirkby Wharfe but never on the finer Anglian monuments, and it is one of the straight-lined patterns which, late in the ninth century, became more and more used, especially in the north. Further, both these crosses have a peculiar kind of plait which is found in Cumberland at St John's (Beckermet), St Bees (Fig. 81), Workington and Plumbland, and especially at Aspatria on a stone bearing the *swastika* which we saw was a mark of the Norse settlers. That is to say,

63

some Cumbrian carver working for the new-comers invented this 'stopped plait', probably taking the hint from metal-work, in which rings of wire, pinched into the semblance of members of double-bead plait, were soldered on the plaque. Stopped plait abandons the old naturalism which regarded the knot as an imitation of plaited cord or thong; but it has a kind of richness in effect of its own, and when carefully executed is not contemptible.

FIGURE 81. ST BEES

Now it is fairly obvious that the Cumberland trick was imported to Whithorn. All but one, perhaps the earliest of the distinctive disc-faced crosses (Fig. 82) characteristic of Whithorn and datable to the second half of the tenth century, use this trick; but there it stays, unaccepted by any other school of carving.

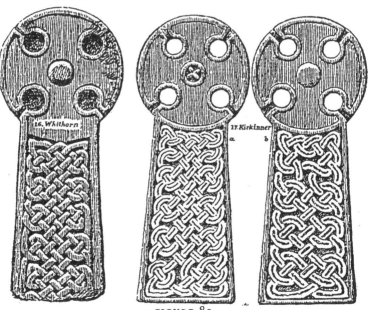

FIGURE 82

64

That the crosses of Fig. 80 were earlier than the disc-faces appears from the heads, with the fan-shaped arms which were already a west-Northumbrian type, but here not regularized into the final penannular form.

These and the disc-faces have simple kinds of plait. The St Ninian's Cave cross shows ring-twist, never seen in the better class of Anglian stones but exceedingly common in the tenth century and later. The 'Donferth' cross is not so well drawn and its plaits are very clumsy, with pellets which are a late feature intended to eke out the effect of poor space-filling. As a frame on one side it has a kind of crest-pattern and on two edges the $T_{L}T$.

The disc-face carver appears to have had a limited stock-in-trade of patterns but he varied them freely and saved his poverty from monotony. Even the ring-twist on the tallest (Fig. 83) of these crosses (now at Sir Herbert Maxwell's, Monreith) is saved by the strong entasis of the shaft which varies the size of the rings; and (perhaps later) he or his school multiplied the rows of rings to three and even four, as on the shaft from Craiglemine at Edinburgh (Fig. 84). Another of his motives was the Carrick bend set horizontally and ladderwise, interwoven with crossing straps; this he also varied, sometimes more, sometimes less, until one almost forgets what a simple formula served for constructing the panel. He used also upright simple twist in parallel rows, crossed and re-crossed with interweaving strands (Fig. 85 shows it both sketched and in relief). A bit of this is seen also at Ilkley Museum as the edge of what must have been a fine cross-head of late Anglian design, showing that the idea is not Celtic. Indeed these disc-faces are by no means Celtic or Scottish. They are derived straight from Anglo-Cumbrian models at a place where Northumbrian tradition was strong, as may be gathered from the fact that the only inscriptions at Whithorn in the tenth century are in the Anglian language. Later on, we could follow these motives as they change under Scottish influence into Celtic forms (Trans. Dumfries and Galloway Ant. Soc. 1925, p. 227) but up to this period no such influence has been felt here. What we learn from these inscribed stones is that in the middle of the tenth century plait-work was no longer the intellectual exercise it was in the eighth, and even in the competent and artistic hands of the Master of the Whithorn series it was based on easy motives, elaborated rather by repetition than by invention.

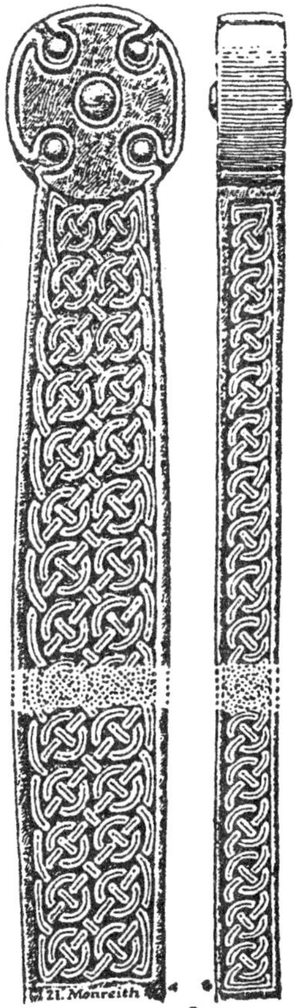

FIGURE 83

To illustrate the course of history by one example more, taking us quite to the end of the pre-Norman age, let us look at the Bingley font (Fig. 86). The inscription has not been interpreted. Dr Vietor offered a reading of a few of the runes, but a careful study of the stone does not make even these few certain, still less the 'Ongus visited Bingley' of Father Haigh (Yorks. Archaeol. Journal, ii, 254) and the 'Eadbierht King let make this dipstone for Ut' of Professor George Stephens ('The runes, whence came they?' 17). The point that seems certain is that these are not Anglian but Scandinavian runes, the style that came into use as early as the tenth century in the Isle of Man, where Gaut Bjarnarson inscribed his work in this way before 950. With minor variations such runes were used in the north of England until late in the twelfth century.

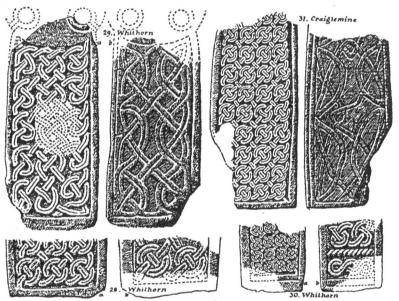

FIGURE 84

The best known examples in stone are the tympanum at Pennington in Furness, which historical considerations place about 1150, when Gamel de Pennington lived, probably the [KA]MIAL of the inscription; the stone in Carlisle Cathedral with 'Dolfin wrote these runes on this stone', about the same time, and the font at Bridekirk (Cumberland) rather later. Two inscriptions in later runes cut on rocks at Barnspike and Hazelgill on the moors above Bewcastle were practical jokes by a neighbour of the Rev. John Maughan, intended to take him in; they were highly successful. But

66

the Bingley runes may be of any time up to the end of the pre-Norman period, including the long overlap when native traditions had not yet given way to the Norman movement; they are likely to be of the twelfth century, when square fonts came into use.

Now consider the plaits on the other side of this stone, and note how they are all derived from what we have seen, but with what a difference! On the south side, the far-away reminiscence of an Anglian scroll, with the berries fallen off the twigs and a ring in the middle. On the north, a thin double-bead strap wandering over the flat

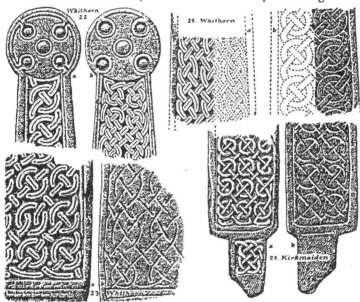

FIGURE 85

ground and not even taking the trouble to go under, where it ought, at its crossing. And on the west, the angular, pelleted plait with a loose member that ends in an apology for leaves, amazingly inept. This was the debasement of pre-Norman pattern somewhere round about 1100; high time for the Norman builders to come in and start fresh.

In this chapter we have run through the examples of plait-work roughly placed in chronology by inscriptions. To summarize the result:—(a) late eighth century and early ninth, complicated, symmetrical and gracefully-flowing lines of interlacements, the pure Anglian school; (b) mid-ninth century, a tendency to use less difficult plaits,

67

which goes with the beginnings of debasement in the animal forms; (c) late ninth century and tenth, the overlap from Anglian to Anglo-Danish, Anglo-Norse, Anglo-Scottish, when much simpler plaits, complicated only by repetition, but making great use of rings and closed members, were the stock-in-trade of the designers of stonework; (d) a kind of renaissance, especially in Northumberland, in the later part of the tenth century, leading to works of some elaboration but not restoring the style of a; and (e) the late eleventh and early twelfth century debasement of pre-Norman art. Of this last, Bingley font is perhaps as degraded an example as we can find, for it occurs in a district with no good traditions. Elsewhere the work was better done, but everywhere the attitude of the designers had changed along with the changes in race, circumstances and general outlook which made Northumbria so kaleidoscopic in the three hundred years before the Norman settlement.

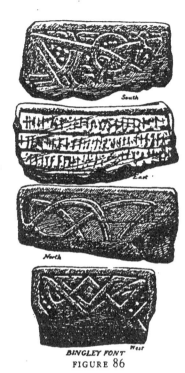

BINGLEY FONT

FIGURE 86

68

Chapter VIII. Anglian Schools of Figure Carving

NORTHUMBRIAN art shows no serious and sustained effort at representing the human figure. The best in this kind are but shadows, and it needs much imagination to amend the worst. And yet there was some attempt in the better times of Anglian stone-carving to present worthy likenesses of worshipful objects. We have seen the saints and angels of St Andrew's, Auckland, and remarked that they look like nascent art in their naturalism, not yet getting hold of a practicable convention in figure drawing. Roman art possessed such a convention, and as long as its traditions lasted there was at any rate the general effect of humanity in its products. But what could be done, even in Roman times, by untrained chippers of stone can be seen in the more grotesque and barbarous figures here and there found along Hadrian's Wall. And as the Anglian carver, uninstructed from without, must have been much in in the same case, it is certain that the Hexham Rood was not his work.

Nor could he learn anything whatever tending to produce the Bewcastle Christ (Fig. 135) or the Ruthwell Annunciation (Fig. 101) from MS. illumination as it was practised early in the eighth century in Northumbria, if we accept the Lindisfarne Gospels as of that date. There is a definite aim at Roman classical ideals in the finer crosses, quite unlike the MS. figure-subjects. Angels indeed have wings, evangelists have books, and every saint has his nimbus; but there the likeness ends. The training and traditions of the stone-carver were certainly not those of the book-illuminator. Some foreign teaching must have stepped in to produce the short-lived school of which two famous works have occupied almost exclusively the attention of critics and antiquaries.

To describe the figure-panels on the Bewcastle and Ruthwell crosses after so many expositions of their subjects and details, so finely illustrated, as have been given by modern writers,* one ought to be prepared to do better. The only fresh point to be raised here is the relation of these carvings to other work in Northumbria, for they do not stand alone and they must be judged by their place in a series, if we can find it.

Now at Easby the piece of a cross-shaft already mentioned (Fig. 53) gives an example of work which in conception and craftsmanship is very closely allied to these great crosses. The seated Christ, holding a book in the left hand and raising the right hand in blessing, has the same sense of representation, with the limbs showing under the fold-skirts, and the same quasi-classic taste in casting the drapery. In one detail it shows better observation than the Christs of Bewcastle and Ruthwell, for the feet are not parallel but turned slightly outwards in a normal attitude. The panel is well filled;

---

* Especially Professor Albert S. Cook in *The Date of the Ruthwell and Bewcastle Crosses*, New Haven, Conn., 1912, and Professor G. Baldwin Brown in *The Arts of Early England*, v, London, 1921. The cast from Bewcastle at Tullie House, Carlisle, is very well seen on its most important side from the landing on the staircase, and favourably lighted by day.

behind the nimbus of Christ are two nimbed heads, possibly the sun and moon, possibly attendant angels; and below, to take the eye off the corner of the frame, are two tendrils of which one still keeps its leaf. The work is a trifle stiffer and coarser than that of Bewcastle and Ruthwell, but it is in the same spirit, inspired by the same teaching; and that teaching has in it the reminiscence of classic Roman sculpture.

Among the stones from Hoddam are two cross-heads (Fig. 51) with figures of Christ in the centre. In one, the half-length figure is framed in a beaded circle with the nimbus and head emerging; the long wavy hair falling on the shoulders and the well-drawn neck with the drapery surrounding it are as at Bewcastle and Ruthwell; the right hand, which holds an open book, is rather more conventional, a little too large, and tending to the stereotyped form (with the first finger separated from the rest) seen both in other stone-work (as the Collingham Apostles) and in manuscripts. In the other cross-head Christ is sitting in a round opening, the head and nimbus as before, but the knees and feet in front of the frame; and there is a good attempt at drawing the knees in a thoroughly classic style, with the drapery properly cast over them. In this figure the hand is again rather large; it is held up in blessing as on the famous crosses. So far as the remainder of these two monuments can be judged from fragments they were of the same type as Ruthwell, with birds and beasts in scrolls and small half-length saints in compartments on the cross-arms.

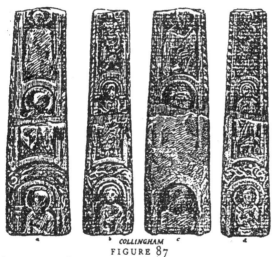

COLLINGHAM

FIGURE 87

At Otley are the fragments of a fine cross (Fig. 52) already partly described. One side was occupied with busts of the four evangelists under arches, each holding his book; and below the four is a panel which has been sadly mutilated but still retains a very beautifully carved head, that of the figure kneeling before the angel. One cannot look at this head without being reminded of Roman treatment. On the other hand the evangelists are, like many Anglian figures, cut out in silhouette with a very deeply sunk ground, so that there is not much left for surface-modelling on the faces, drapery and hands; but this lower panel seems to have been attempted in classic relief, such as lasted in Roman sculpture to the sixth century, and in the eighth was supplanted in

Italy by the general use of the strongly-outlined, shallow-detailed style which late Anglian figures illustrate. At Otley we seem to have the two treatments side by side; the evangelists were perhaps carved by one man, the angel by another, and the two carvers were brought up under different influences.

The two early schools seem to be that of the St Andrew's, Auckland, figures (Fig. 50) and that of the Bewcastle and Ruthwell crosses. In one sense, all relief-carving must be done under some kind of convention, to make it possible; but the Auckland saints and angels look as though the artist had no preconceived and ready-made technical method. He had a formula, though, which was exactly this of the Otley evangelists, the flattish figure strongly outlined on a deep-sunk ground. And this makes it con-

ceivable that he was simply a-dopting the manner in vogue during the eighth century in Italy, while another group of carvers took classic sculpture as their model. Now we have seen that the Hexham builders had no use for the antique; they built it in. Any such school as appreciated the modelling of a classic relief must have come into action later than that time. Bede tells us (*Hist. Eccl.* iv. 19) of the use of a ready-made sarcophagus, no doubt Roman, for a Christian burial, so that if there had been an objection to the pagan monument it was overruled. The people at Carlisle in 685

HODDAM

FIGURE 88

showed St Cuthbert their Roman antiquities, to which he gave no great attention; at the moment he was occupied with higher things—his vision of Ecgfrith's overthrow at Nechtansmere. But St Cuthbert was of the old order: in the eighth century, travel to Italy had been more frequently repeated; Acca was importing adornments to his church (perhaps the Rood, a good piece of figure-carving); and the door was open to a master-sculptor who knew and admired Roman art and taught pupils to work in a classic style. At the same time, we gather, others were at work in what was then the 'modern' style, the flat relief of strongly-outlined figures. They may have argued that this was more decorative, broader, more effective; there are always reasons; but that the two schools coexisted the Otley cross appears to indicate.

71

The 'modern' style, of course, carried the day. If the Collingham 'Apostles' (Fig. 87) is early ninth century, it exhibits the fruits of the 'modernist' movement. It is not work of a very skilful draughtsman; the figures are not well proportioned; the hands in two instances are like the Hoddam hand; but there is a good deal of life and a distinct attempt at variety of attitude and character, as in the Auckland saints. With that

we class the Hoddam and Heysham 'dolls' houses' (Figs. 88, 89), much better carved than the Collingham shaft, but in the same general style as to means of effect, and Fig. 88 with the same hands. The faces are not portrait-like, nor ideal; the composition is not based on swinging curves, nor

HEYSHAM

FIGURE 89

has it the logic of a great tradition. We are now in the early ninth century: there has been time for the teaching of the originators of the two rival schools to have been diluted by two or three generations of pupils, and the law of art-history bids us look for decadence.

DEWSBURY

FIGURE 90

72

Meanwhile the classic school has not quite died out. The Hovingham slab (Fig. 54), though it is so worn that details are debatable, shows at any rate the very graceful angel of the Annunciation and the pretty figure of the Virgin on her camp-stool; and all the rest must have been in the tradition of classic charm, as one gathers from the flow of outline still visible. Less plainly we seem to see this in the Masham column (Fig. 55); it is so weathered that details have gone, but still there is design in the groups and the lines are flowing, the proportions are not grotesque; one can believe that the carver had not forgotten the precepts of a teacher who said, like old Crome, 'Whatever you do, my boy, dignify it.'

In this Masham stone, second tier, is a figure reading in front of a small arch. So on the Cundall-Aldborough shaft (Fig. 32) some figure, now defaced, was under a small arch.

We infer (p. 45) that both these stones by their provenance must have been of a Ripon school. Further down the Cundall shaft is a little group in architectural surroundings, of which the carving has been delicate and on a very small scale. We have already suspected the existence of a Ripon school in the first half of the ninth century, neat-handed at miniature sculpture. It is neither the bold work of the 'classic' school nor the somewhat crude work of the 'modernists', but a new style. To what height of daintiness and finish it could rise is seen in the Hornby stone (Fig. 71) with its almost virginal Christ and apostle at the Miracle of the Loaves and Fishes, and its neat little angel on the reverse.

Following on the lines of this school but a generation later comes the group of men — for no doubt the master, as always, had his assistants — who carved the great Paulinus cross at Dewsbury. Their aims were by this time eclectic, but their powers in decadence. The Christ (Fig. 90a) has very distinct likeness to the seated figure at Hoddam; the knees are shown, but there is no figure inside the drapery and the whole design is far gone in decay. The drapery of the saints among the arches interests the carver, but not for its likeness to real cloth or for the beautiful forms it can take. The little Madonna (Fig. 91d), under her own small arch, is engaging because she is the first of her kind in English stone, but she is not a great triumph of art; nor are the figures in the Miracles. They have some expression; the Virgin is saying to Christ, 'They have no wine', and He blesses the waterpots while St John presses his hand to his cheek in wonderment. Below, Christ reaches out to multiply the loaves and fishes and the disciples behind look on, trying to strain round and peep at the working of the miracle. It is all lively and dramatic, but very poor sculpture. The Ripon school of a generation earlier would have done the work with greater skill and neatness; and one proof of decadence is the deep drill-hole in every eye, intended to hold a bit of bright glass or crystal and give a sparkle in the midst of the network of colour which was pretty certainly added to the carving and, to the eye of the public, covered deficiencies. 'Since you could not make her fair,' said Apelles, 'you make her fine.'

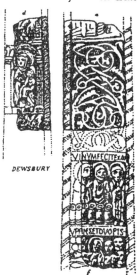

DEWSBURY

FIGURE 91

Halton, in Lonsdale, a few miles up the Lune from Lancaster, is a site which must have been of some importance in pre-Norman days, and in Norman times also, for it possesses one of the mottes which usually denote a lordship. In the churchyard is the 'Sigurd' shaft, of which there will be more to say in treating the later period. Upon this has been placed in recent times some stones of a fine Anglian cross. Inside the

73

church are preserved a number of interesting fragments, two groups of which are built up into a couple of shafts (Fig. 92). The first has at the top the figure of a seated saint with cross and book, drawn and carved very much in the style of the Dewsbury 'Paulinus' figures. Beneath is an angel, nimbed and winged, holding a great tablet or Book of Remembrance on which may have been the inscription. At the angel's feet is a little crouching figure, as on the top of the Paulinus cross and resembling — though not nearly so well done — the monk kneeling to the angel at Otley. Below this in another arch are the remains of two heads; the rest of the panel is lost; but allowing for the missing part we can fit into the shaft, lower down, a stone with the same cable-edging and a flock of sheep. It might be suggested that the lost panel represented Christ's charge to St Peter, and that Peter is the saint portrayed above. This monument finds its place in the series at about the level of Dewsbury great cross, a little before the Danish invasion had made its influence felt.

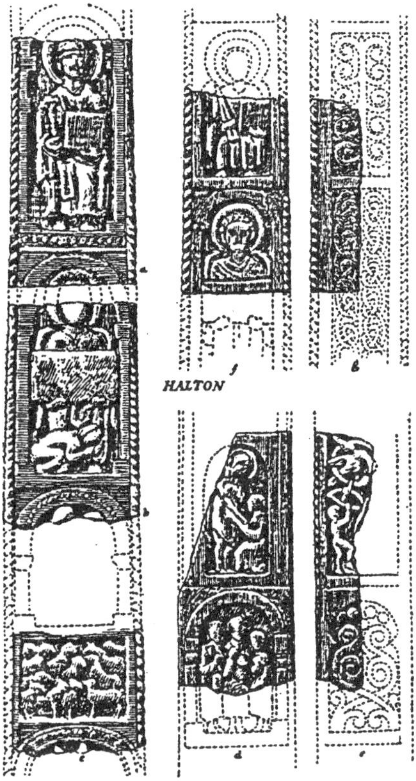

The Danish settlement did not include this district. It is likely that work went on afterwards, though in decadent circumstances. And so, when we find (f) a second shaft, obviously imitating the first, it must be of the Anglian survival. There is the saint again; the fold of drapery under his right hand has become part of the sword (or whatever it was) which he holds. The angel is there too, quaintly debased. And the patterns on the adjacent side (g) of the stone are a late tree-scroll and the very common late loop-twist (Romilly Allen's no. 653) seen first at Melsonby, then at Dewsbury and often in the tenth century, confirming our impression.

HALTON

FIGURE 92

The third stone (de) must belong to another monument because the cable-edging is different. Its carving seems to rank it with the first (abc) rather than so late as the second (fg), but the coarse, flat-strap pelleted scroll can only mean decadence of Anglian style. In two arched panels it has figure-subjects; Christ and a kneeling woman,

74

perhaps Mary and her risen Lord, and three figures holding rolled books or scrolls which may, as elsewhere, represent the Three Children in the Furnace. On the side, much broken, is an archer, as at Ruthwell and Auckland.

The Archer appears again (Fig. 93) in the stone at Sheffield (a cast is in the Weston Museum at that town) which is possibly part of the great cross in the churchyard pulled down in 1570, when fourpence was paid for the job and the stones were 'solde to George Tynker' for a shilling (The Reliquary, xiii, 204-208); Mr C. F. Innocent of Sheffield, however, informs the writer that the stone may have been brought by a former owner from Derbyshire. On this stone are late patterns; a coarsened Anglian scroll, and the plait (Romilly Allen's no. 638) which occurs at Ripon, Chester-le-Street, Durham, St Andrew's, Sandbach, Bakewell, Knook (Wilts.) and in South Wales; not one that is known on early stones, but associated with tenth century work. In this case the plait runs into a tree-scroll, and the combination on one panel (like the mixed plaits of Thornhill, Dumfriesshire) suggests the effort to vary older forms. The archer is very well drawn; the work of a clever man but obviously not bred in the earlier schools, for instead of traditional drapery this figure wears the ordinary kirtle, hose and shoes of the day and uses the little bow of the Anglo-Saxon hunter. It is interesting to notice that the designer entirely forgot that his cross was to be set up on end, and drawing the figure as the stone

a   *b*   *c*

SHEFFIELD

FIGURE 93

lay on the ground he has left his archer shinning up the frame. The tapering of the stone forbids us to regard it as a lintel; it must be a cross-shaft. This curious carelessness is not without analogies though always in late work, beginning perhaps with the fox at Ilkley (Fig. 49*n*) and seen notably in the Gosforth cross (Fig. 184). An oversight of this kind surely argues the decadence. The Sheffield cross is Anglian in derivation of motives but hardly dates before the tenth century. It is pretty certainly a product of the school of Bakewell.

This carries us to the end of the Anglian tradition in the south, not counting a few odds and ends, such as the saint on the shortest cross at Ilkley church (Fig. 61), the bishop at Crofton (Fig. 64) and traces of a rather large figure at Hackness (Fig. 75).

We have indeed followed the clue farther than the time when the Danes destroyed the abbeys in central Yorkshire and county Durham, and with them the schools or firms of craftsmen depending on the abbeys. But while the Danes were 'debacchantes', as old writers put it, in Yorkshire, it can hardly be doubted that some of the craftsmen took refuge in the west in and in the north just as the bearers of St Cuthbert's relics did. Beyond the Tyne, after the first ravaging of 875, the Anglian state recovered

ROTHBURY

FIGURE 94

itself and continued in existence with diminished glory and in straitened circumstances, and still there were churches and still there was demand for monuments.

Now we have not yet mentioned a few pieces in the north that show a definite Anglian tradition, but as we take it, late Anglian. Of these the finest is the Rothbury cross (Figs. 94, 95). Some fragments are at the Blackgate Museum in Newcastle-upon-Tyne;* these were taken out of the fabric of the church and are in a very crisp condition compared with the piece which remains as font-pedestal at Rothbury. Many are the sins of church-restorers, but to them we owe such a wealth of monuments, carrying history back beyond the twelfth century building-age, that there is surely a place for forgiveness.

* A reconstruction of the whole cross and full illustrations of the parts are given by Mr C. C. Hodges in 'Archaeologia Aeliana', 1925. Excellent photographs have been taken of these and other pieces by Mr John Gibson, F.S.A., of Hexham.

The pieces give the head and foot of the cross. If all pre-Norman shafts were straight-sided it would be easy to determine the height by continuing the taper of the lowest fragment to meet the head. But in many cases and especially as time went on, the cross-designers found that an entasis or slight outward curve in the outline (as in classical columns) took off a certain stiffness in effect and added to the appearance of height by a kind of perspective illusion. With the entasis the whole monument might be about fourteen feet from the base, the height of the beautiful Gosforth cross. Ruthwell cross was about seventeen feet high.

The plait at the foot ought to give us some help towards the period. It is apparently unique and overlooked by Romilly Allen*, but it is akin to the Lindisfarne and Durham

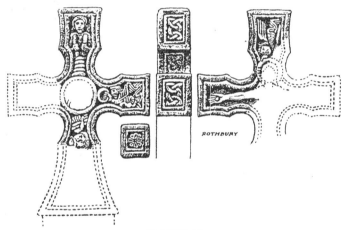

FIGURE 95

plaits in general character and extremely different from those of Bewcastle. At Bewcastle one is struck by the designer's aim in working the whole panel together into a composition of swinging lines; not merely patterning it over with 'repeats'. Here at Rothbury one sees 'repeats' filling the panel but capable of filling a longer panel by additions, if it had been desired, like a wall-paper. That could not be done with a Bewcastle plait, which would need to be completely re-designed if the shape of the frame were altered. Now this means a different way of considering the problem of space-filling, and one that shirks the difficulties faced by designers of the best period.

* Who in a letter long ago explained to the writer that he had not intended to list every known plait, but only those which had to do with Celtic monuments. Still, his catalogue of analogies remains a useful basis for a study that needs much attention by any student of crosses. What Dragendorff forms are to the Roman digger, plait forms are to our subject.

It means decadence, not so far gone as the very cheap rings and twists of the poorer tenth century work, but a good many steps in that direction.

The scrolls, figures and animals of Rothbury, though the work of a distinctly efficient carver, tell the same tale. In some respects, as in the drilled eye-pupils and the deeply sunk ground, they are like the work of the Paulinus cross, though better carved; they are unlike the Ruthwell cross in a certain bluntness and want of spring in the curves, not to say that the motives are entirely different in character. Instead of the early fruit-pecking birds and playful little beasts we have uncouth and unpettable creatures, writhing and biting in a nightmare of tangles. The south side of the lower stone, with its inhuman torso at the foot, holding the legs of the pig-like monsters, and the hobgoblins at the top, one of them a mere head with fingers holding the slimy dragon-tails apart to look through, would have been impossible to the kindly fancy of an eighth century Northumbrian. Possibly this is a recollection of the gripping-beast style of Scandinavia and the savage motives of ornament imported from over the sea, but not carved by a Dane or Norseman, who would have forsaken that style long before; and yet they taint the tradition of the Anglian beast. On this panel there are beast-heads not in profile: that we have already seen at Melsonby; but the Melsonby creatures were still graceful. That the Rothbury carver was skilful does not tell his date; that is settled by the double outline and scaly backs, which cannot be earlier than 900 and may be considerably later.

FIGURE 96

At Dewsbury, in the Loaves and Fishes panel (Fig. 91) we had the first beginnings of a crowd of people, and the flock of sheep is seen at Halton. At Rothbury we have two crowds, one of little heads (souls in heaven?) looking down from the top of the shaft at the scene (lost to us) below, and another of apostles looking awkwardly up from the foot of the shaft at Christ ascending. We have refused evidence from MSS. and we still refuse it; but that pictures of such crowds were visible is likely, and everyone will remember the well-known page of the Benedictional of St Ethelwold (about 975) with this subject. It must have been familiar in the tenth century. Crowds, indeed, were drawn earlier, as in the German psalter given by King Æthelstan to St Cuthbert's shrine; but this crowd at Rothbury does not reproduce the scene in that book, nor indeed that in the Benedictional at Chatsworth; it only tells us that this cross is a distinctly late piece of design by the fact of its attempting to portray a crowd.

Finally let us call attention to the ribbed drapery, both in the Christ at the top of the shaft and in the Healing of the

78

Blind Man on the side adjacent. It is very unlike Anglian drawing of folds; something like the curious figure with the barrel, found at Corstopitum; though possibly the parallel lines of the cloak in the Auckland panel of angels, or other work of late Roman derivation, suggested this treatment. But for a close analogy there is the Hunter at Jarrow (Fig. 96). His coat is all ribs; the beast and the scroll with knops of fruit, are closely like the Rothbury beasts and scroll; and the deep cutting is similar to that of the cross in Fig. 95. It is most likely that the two birds in a tree-scroll at Jarrow are part of the Hunter monument; they too resemble the Rothbury work, especially in the symmetrical and wormy boughs.

If we attribute these to the tenth century, as all the indications suggest, it may be objected that there was no abbey in the neighbourhood to account for so important and accomplished an effort. Still however, the district was Christian. The 'Historia de Sancto Cuthberto', attributed the time of King Cnut (Surtees Society, vol. li, 147 ff.) has much to say about ecclesiology in county Durham and Northumberland during the tenth century, in spite of Ragnvald the Viking (912) and that *filius diaboli*, Olaf Ball (the stubborn). That there were churches and sufficient wealth to support them is evident and accounts for the very large number of late Anglian monuments, some of them attributable to the monastery at Durham founded 995, some to an earlier church of St Oswald there, but others to churches on old abbey sites and elsewhere all over the district.

AYCLIFFE

FIGURE 97

As samples of this style, later in general aspect than Eadulf's cross from Alnmouth (Fig. 79), we might take a shaft at Aycliffe, co. Durham (Fig. 97) and one of several similar cross-heads at Durham itself. Aycliffe, anciently Heaclif, was granted by bishop

79

Ealdhun with his daughter Ecgfrida (one need not hesitate over the statement, but suppose him married, like bishop Strickland of Carlisle, before taking orders) in marriage to Uchtred son of Waltheof, earl of Northumberland, about 997. Details can be read in the tract 'De Obsessione Dunelmi' (Surtees Soc., vol. li, 154ff). It was not church property but no doubt possessed a church, as many vills did by that time. So things went on, the place being of value to owners ranking as earls, until the great Siward was dead and then '*werra surgente*, those lands were devasted'. This gives a reason for inferring that the Aycliffe crosses, and there are a dozen various fragments known, may have been put up—not to commemorate two synods supposed to have been held there in 783 and 789—but as gravestones when the place was the demesne of a bishop or an earl, late

DURHAM

FIGURE 98

tenth century to early eleventh. With such a period the style agrees. This stone bears two Scandinavian dragons and two panels of basket-plait, which means tenth century ornament. It has two knots, the upper found elsewhere only at Chester-le-Street, founded in 900, and Durham, founded 995; and the other common to Durham, Abercorn, St Andrews (Fife) and several late Anglian places in Yorkshire. Its figure subjects are two Crucifixions, one of Christ, with Longinus and the Sponge-bearer represented grotesquely, as in late crosses (in this case as obese dwarfs), and the other of St Peter, head downwards. It has also two pairs and two triplets of figures. The triplets hold books; one set are nimbed but not the other; and they are crossed in front by the bar which is often seen on County Durham figure-groups but does not seem to be explained unless these, as at Halton, are the Three Children in the fiery furnace. In this rude though laboured carving, a certain amount of Anglian tradition is obvious, but still further concessions than at Rothbury are made to Danish motives; and all that can be called real figure drawing has disappeared.

The cross-head at Durham (Fig. 98) is one of four, taken from the foundation of the Chapter House commenced not long after 1100 and finished in 1140; the Norman builders thought them *rudes et idiotae*; no wonder. But they have value to us when we regard them as documents telling facts about the founders of Durham abbey in 995

80

and their last despairing clutch at the ancient Anglian tradition. The Lamb in the cross-centre we have seen at Hoddam, about two hundred years earlier, drawn from a classical model. The angel above, the winged ox and lion on the lateral arms, and the eagle at the top of the other side no doubt mean the evangelists, as seen on such Anglian crosses as at Otley. There are angels and saints, and the scene of Christ's baptism with St John ladling the water and, to fill a circle, a strange figure ending downwards in an egg-shape; and its hair in one of the repeats is long. It has puzzled the antiquaries. Does it mean a mermaid, to signify water? If that is so, here is a far-away reminiscence of the classic Roman symbol. But there is very little left, now, of classic derivation, although we have traced the downward path step by step from the dignity of the Easby Christ to this. What kind of man can bishop Ealdhun have been? What sort of things made him laugh, if he ever did? And poor Ecgfrida. Well, she died in odour of sanctity after being twice married to great lords and twice sent home to her father. But what could angels and saints mean to a nun who saw them drawn like this?

If we did not know what strange things are accepted from time to time as Art, we might think that such examples were likely to bring religion into contempt, except that imagination amends them. Only, knowing the facts, we can no longer attribute the fine Anglian crosses to people who tolerated the nightmares of the tenth century and the caricatures of the eleventh.

Chapter IX. The Free-Armed Head

ALL Anglian crosses that have any heads left are free-armed. All cut-out wheel-heads are of the later, Anglo-Danish and Anglo-Norse period. Those wheel-crosses that are incised or in relief on standing slabs (the Celtic type which must be distinguished from the tall monument carved out in silhouette) are not found in the Northumbrian region except on post-Conquest grave slabs. And further, the 'Celtic' crosses seen on slabs at Hartlepool and elsewhere are never cut out in the round to surmount the Anglian shaft.

Anglian cross-heads begin with the forms on St Cuthbert's coffin and his pectoral cross minus the little bosses in the armpits of the latter. (If the reader will allow the use of 'armpits' for the re-entrant angles or curves at the intersections of the cross-arms, a

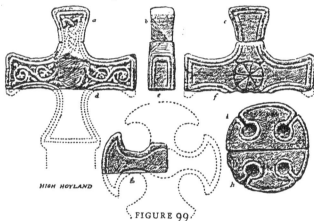

HIGH HOYLAND

FIGURE 99.

certain amount of pedantic circumlocution can be avoided.) These little bosses appear most unexpectedly in the late wheel-heads of Chester and West Kirby; at Middleton near Pickering and Kirklevington free-armed crosses have a cylinder or roll inserted into each armpit which gives the same effect; but otherwise the normal Anglian cross has rounded and uninterrupted armpits, subject to variations in the outline of the cross as a whole.

The purest example of the 'pectoral' type is the Northallerton head (Fig. 30) with chevrons and Ormside Cup ornament. It seems to be of the Ripon school, and roughly of 820 or thereabouts. The Acca cross was very likely of this form; it restores most conveniently so (Fig. 38) but we cannot be certain. This normal form is often found carved in relief, as on the Wensley slabs (Fig. 17, *b, c*) and more rarely standing free, as at High Hoyland (Fig. 99, *a, c*) somewhat coarsened. It is difficult to cut in the round if the

82

grace of the curves and the slenderness of the arms are to be preserved; therefore, the 'coffin' form (as in Fig. 72) was commonly used; the arms were made shorter and thicker, though the armpits were still considered as sweeping curves, not merely little round bites taken out of the stone as if the shape were a four-holed wheel-head with the wheel knocked off. This last is the 'Celtic' form, seen in England only at very late periods (Fig. 17e).

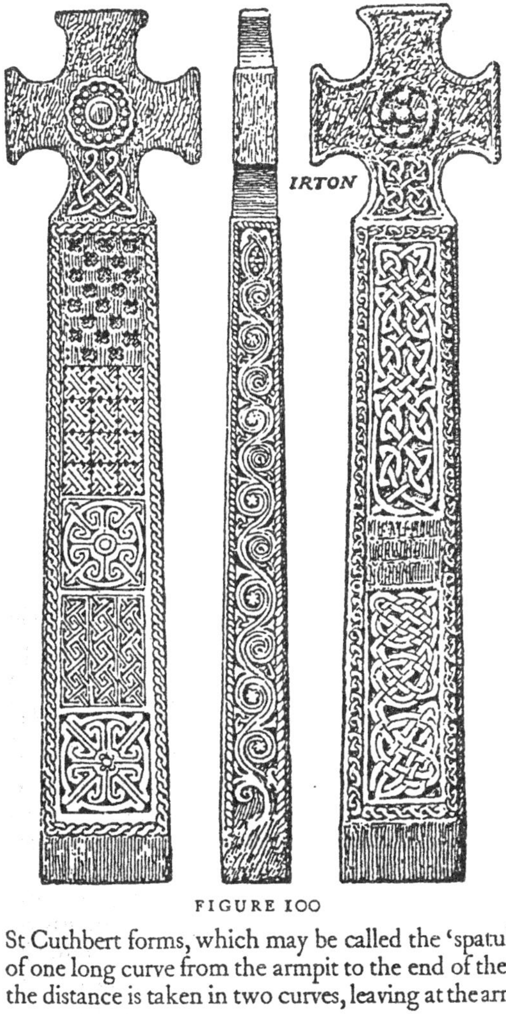

FIGURE 100

The coarsened 'pectoral' shape occurs in the fine cross (Fig. 100) at Irton (West Cumberland) where perhaps its out-of-the-way site accounts for its wonderful preservation. It is a very late but entirely Anglian type. Early runes, said to have been seen by Father Haigh in 1863, on the three bands of the blank panel, cannot now be read; but what is known of them agrees with the design. On the edges are good scrolls; the plaits, key-pattern, and blocks of square-planned ornament resemble those we attribute to the tenth century in Northumberland and county Durham, while the group of bosses at the cross-centre on the west side connects with the Lancaster school. The uppermost panel on the east seems to be an elaboration of the chequers of Bewcastle. An eclectic work of the Anglian survival.

At a very early period however, there was a variant on the St Cuthbert forms, which may be called the 'spatulated' head. That is to say, instead of one long curve from the armpit to the end of the arm, or a curve and a straight line, the distance is taken in two curves, leaving at the arm-end a fairly broad 'spade' prettily

83

tapered with curved outlines. This was rather easier than the 'pectoral' to cut because the curves were not so long and did not need such very accurate measurement nor such precaution against breaking the stone. It lent itself to varied ornament on the cross-arms; it gave also an interesting silhouette, seen against the sky. But this form, which was especially used in very large crosses, was also breakable. When the stones were used for building the first thing the Vandals did was to knock off the arms and use them as rubble; then to chip off the boss from the centre and make that part lie flat in the stone-course; and so we have a number of spatulated-head fragments but no complete head of this type. The nearest to completion is from Rothbury (Fig. 95) a poor, late example, for the armpit-curve is too small and sharp; but the fragment shows how we can restore the spatulated arms found at Lastingham (two, Fig. 133, one very large), Masham (two, Fig. 133, representing two large cross-heads), Dewsbury (the Angel, Fig. 73), Hoddam (three, Fig. 51), and Halton (now set on the top of the churchyard cross). That this type survived until the eleventh century is shown by Durham crosses (Fig. 98), a Dewsbury head with the plain ground ornamented only with moulding-lines and cable (Fig. 106n), and the still plainer example found at Ilkley in 1921 during the digging of the Roman fort close to the church.

The Ruthwell cross (Fig. 101) was of this form. When the cross was re-erected the restorer (most forgivably, for it was more than a hundred years ago) put in a new piece which does not quite fit the main armpit-curve and leaves little cusps where no cusps ought to be. But we can

FIGURE IOI

84

easily see that by enlarging the curves of the restored head a little, as drawn in the illustration, we get a slightly bigger head of a very graceful form, true to type. Very much trouble and ingenuity have been spent by Dr King Hewison and his friends in measuring and considering the fragments with a view to restoring the cross as a wheel-head; but there is no certain indication of any remains of the spring of the wheel which ought to be found on the upper and lower fragments, if there were any originally. The three cuts he mentions are too low down for the place where the wheel would meet the neck;

they seem only to mean damage to the offset at the base of the head, which is usual in a spatulated cross, and would be trimmed off by the mason when he re-used the stone. This offset meant at first the attempt to turn the rain from the joint, when (as almost inevitable in great crosses) the head was a separate stone dowelled to the shaft. It became a regular feature, preserved in many cases when a smaller monument was carved out of one stone, or even when it was represented in relief, as seen in the Wensley slabs. This must have been the type adopted at Ruthwell, as in so many of the greater and more ambitious of Anglian monuments.

Bewcastle cross must have had a head (Fig. 102) made of a separate stone and dowelled to the shaft; the socket-hole remains, and part of the head, though now lost, is on record. The story of this fragment is told

Suggestion for head of
BEWCASTLE CROSS
W. G. C. 1921.

FIGURE 102

by the late Canon James Wilson, of Dalston, in the Cumberland and Westmorland Society's Transactions for 1910, and has often been re-told—how Lord William Howard of Naworth in 1608 showed it to Sir Henry Spelman and Camden the antiquary, and then sent it to Sir Robert Cotton, who made a note (facsimile in Fig. 103) of the runes upon it and described its dimensions but omitted to sketch its form. One thing is certain; it could not have been the whole cross-head but only a bit of the uppermost arm, for it measured no more than 16 inches high, 12 inches broad at the top and four inches thick. Spelman called it the *epistylium* of the cross; and here we venture to

85

suggest an alternative theory to that offered by Professor Baldwin Brown ('Arts in Early England', v, 115 ff.). In the use of the word *epistylium* we need not see the equivalent of 'impost'. The Oxford Dictionary quotes a writer of about 1623, close to the date of Cotton's note, thus: — '160 Pillars of Stone, whose Epistylia, or Chapiters were wrought about in fashion of a Crowne'. In this, *Epistylia* can hardly mean anything but 'capitals'; and the Jacobean antiquaries probably took the fragment for the capital or summit of the whole monument. A sketch to scale shows how it would work in as part of the great cross-head, with the runes, as at Ruthwell, cut on the frame. The fracture, when the head was blown down by a gale, as tradition relates, would occur at the narrow part of the arm, and the length of the fragment (16 inches) hints the

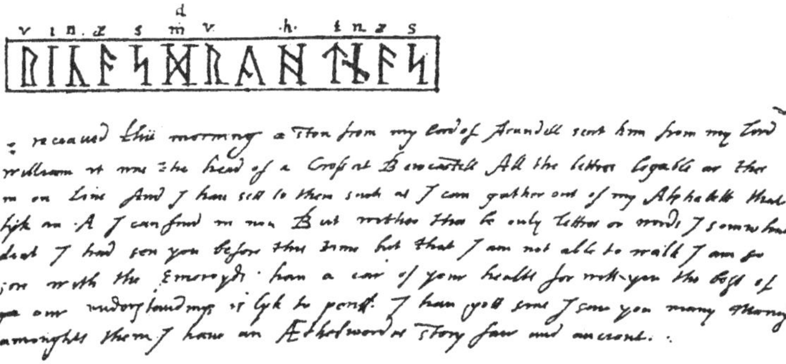

FIGURE 103

approximate size of the head. Its width (12 inches) gives the dimensions of the cross-arms, and its thickness (4 inches), together with the fact that no carving seems to have appeared at the back, suggests that the stone was flaked or split off from an original thickness of about 8 inches, which would be required in so large a cross-head. This splitting is highly probable when we remember that early cross-carvers were not usually experienced in quarrying: they did not always get the best piece of stone, and sometimes they face-bedded their block; that is, placed it so that the natural bait (cleavage or bedding) was vertical. The rain then worked into fissures, at first imperceptible, and enlarged them; frost split the crest of the stone, and nature began the work of destruction. This is seen in several instances; one very remarkable is the West Kirby hogback in which the weathering of a face-bedded block is striking. If the suggestion here offered has anything in it, we can see the Bewcastle cross complete, and true to the Northumbrian type, at any rate a sister to Ruthwell as the rest of its design would show it to be. We must read the runes RICÆS DRYHTNÆS.

The spatuled head had its debasements. In the stone from Middleton Hall affixed to

86

the tallest cross at Ilkley church (Fig. 63) one sees the type already a little the worse for want of care in striking the armpit curves and hollowing the edges of the blocks which form the ends of the arms; and the late period of that head is obvious. The St Cuthbert's coffin type also could be debased, making the arm-end a heavy oblong block. And as in reconsideration this rectangularity must have seemed inharmonious with the taper of the shaft, in many cases the blocks at the arm-ends were slightly bevelled or splayed off: for example, the Carlisle head (Fig. 104) with scroll and chevron, a piece

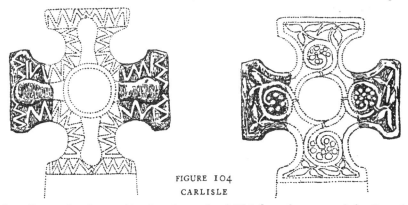

FIGURE 104
CARLISLE

of Anglian work influenced by the Ripon school. This form also was carried on into the survival and appears at Gainford (Durham Cathedral Library, No. xxiii); and in very late examples the splay was exaggerated, the block enlarged, until such 'Celtic' forms were produced as the Kirkdale Crucifix (Fig. 126), the head with pelleted *triquetrae* at Sinnington, and Kirkby Grindalythe cross which we have reason to date twelfth century (Fig. 217).

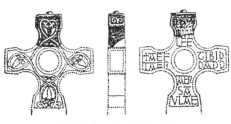

FIGURE 105. CARLISLE

St Cuthbert's pectoral cross had necessarily a little knob at the top, to hold the cord or chain by which it hung round the neck. This we see reproduced in the 'Badwulf' cross at Carlisle (Fig. 105) good Anglian; we see it again, considerably later, in the crucifix of Kirkburton near Huddersfield (Fig. 125) and the debased head at Wath near Ripon. Twelfth century Irish crosses have something similar in the form of a little house at the top of the whole, but there is no obvious connexion between this development and the Northumbrian knob.

87

Reverting now to the variations on the ordinary type we find that late Anglian designers tried to make it more fanciful by enlarging the arms into a fan-shape. This trick is illustrated in the Dewsbury heads (Fig. 106), a ninth century spatulated form and a later, plain example of the same, with a late fan-armed head. Kirkby Wharfe has two examples, of which the earliest (Fig. 107) has the T⌊T but a passably drawn pair of figures, SS. Mary and John beside the Cross, with a bit of leafage springing from the superimposed cross-arms, which suggests Anglian tradition not very advanced in decay. The fan-shape is also not strongly marked; it is just a trifle more pronounced in the other Kirkby Wharfe example, of which the trellis ornament indicates the end of the tenth century. There is another example at Collingham and a fourth at Saxton, all with the

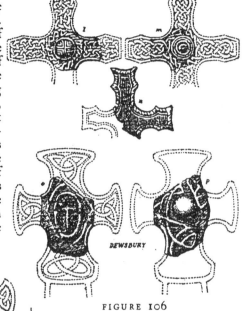

FIGURE 106

KIRKBY, WHARFE

88   FIGURE 107

same centre pattern, remarkable because Gaut Bjarnarson used it in the Isle of Man. At Tadcaster is the arm of a similar cross, the centre lost. At Finghall, up Wensleydale, is a crucifix-head with similar arms; not much expanded. But at Staveley, between Aldborough and Knaresborough, and at Burnsall (Fig. 108), far up Wharfedale, are crosses in which the fan-shape is very pronounced, and the ornament is of a Scandinavian type (see on Fig. 190) which makes them as late as 1000 or beyond. The outlier of the group is at

Sherburn, east of Malton, where all the work seems late tenth to eleventh century. In the south of Yorkshire High Hoyland (Fig. 99) shows a curious arm which may have belonged to a head of this form, plain and without anything but moulding lines and no doubt eleventh century at earliest.

Crossing the Pennines westward, there is a head at Kirkby Stephen (Fig. 109) tending to this type but of Anglian tradition; perhaps earlier than mid-tenth century. At Gressingham on the Lune above Lancaster is a well-marked example neatly carved with regular plaits and not unlike another at Aughton in south Lanca-

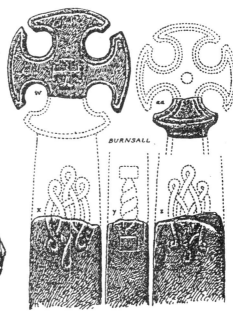

FIGURE 108

FIGURE 109. KIRKBY STEPHEN

shire. The cross at Bolton-le-Moors (Lancs.) is quite of the latest Anglian character; a fan-armed head at Whalley has on one side only moulding-lines, and the ugly head (Fig. 221) from Cheadle (Cheshire) in the Philosophical Society's Museum at York (Hospitium, No. 17) bears the debased apology for ornament which marks the latest pre-Norman age. We have already remarked Anglian forms in what is now Scotland but once part of Northumbria, and it is no surprise to see a cross-head of this type from Glencairn at the Grierson Museum, Thornhill (Dumfriesshire). From this series we gather that the type lasted all through

89

the eleventh century, starting perhaps early in the tenth; and that it was evolved from the old Anglian cross-form is evident.

The Sherburn and Burnsall examples, with the tips of the fans blunted, prepare us for curious forms at High Hoyland (Fig. 99) and Bakewell. In these the fan-arms have been so much expanded that they look as if they had grown like plants until they pressed against each other and flattened their points. The High Hoyland stone, only half the head, appears to have been split, and the two sides are now built into the church wall simulating a complete head; and that head is exactly like the Whithorn disc-face (Fig. 82). It would be most difficult to believe that there is no connexion; not that the Whithorn carver actually borrowed straight from Bakewell or *vice versa*, but the type was known in the middle of the tenth century, no doubt in more places than those where specimens happen to be visible. The Whithorn disc-face, we have already remarked, seems to be derived from the fan-shaped arms of the Anglo-Cumbrian crosses (Fig. 80) seen there, and they can hardly be much earlier or much later than about 950, because they have the T↓T but also have Anglian names and runes.

SPENNITHORNE

FIGURE 110

At Dover is a well-known grave-slab with runes seeming to read 'Gislheard'. There was a bishop of Selsey named Gislhere dating about 775 to 784, but we have been warned against attributing inscribed monuments to historical persons, and in this case the names are not even identical. The first rune in the name is that which we saw beginning 'Gilsuith' on the Thornhill (Yorks.) stone, late ninth century; and the form of the cross on the Dover slab is a development of the fan-shape arm, in which the uppermost member is greatly exaggerated. It can hardly be earlier than the regular fan-arms; probably tenth century. Now this exaggeration of the topmost arm is seen in much the same shape on a grave-slab (Fig. 110) at Spennithorne (Wensleydale) with bifurcated plaits, which means Anglo-Danish; no bifurcations are seen in right Anglian work. And yet the Dover runes are right Anglian; we have to balance the one against the other and we get this apparently late development of the fan-shaped arms not late in the tenth century, which shows the possibility of the type somewhat earlier.

Similar to this exaggerated upper arm but evolved out of the 'coffin' type coarsened is the last important group of free-armed heads—the ugly hammer-head seen in relief on a shaft at Gargrave in Craven (Fig. 111) with pelleted plaits and highly debased scrolls of the eleventh century. In Yorkshire it is cut out in the round at Middlesmoor, up Nidderdale, with the very latest kind of debased ornament and curious lettering (Fig. 112). If we turn the stone as it lay while it was being carved and read the lines, with much allowance for the illiteracy of a carver in the worst period, we can make out ✠/CROS/SCE CE/✠ADA, with the D crossed, — 'The cross of St Ceada' or Chad; not that this was his gravestone, but a memorial in a place dedicated to him in the eleventh century. The church at Middlesmoor was consecrated 1484; nothing earlier is known; but it is quite impossible to assign this ugly thing either to that late period or to nascent Anglian art, and we have a late pre-Norman series in which it finds its place (Chap. XVII).

Earlier than this are the Carlisle cross (Fig. 116-7) with the hammerhead and spine-and-boss pattern, and that at Dearham (Cumberland) with spine-and-boss and Cumbrian leafless spirals (Fig. 116-10). Another hammerhead at Brigham on the Cumberland Derwent, without ornament, seems to represent eleventh century work. This dating is supported by the rude hammerhead (Fig. 116-14) with a late and debased wheel, also with Cumbrian spirals, at Addingham (Cumberland) and by the slab, carved on both sides but not cut out in the round, from the ruined chapel at Kilmorie and now at Corsewall House in Kirkcolm in the north of the Rhynns of Galloway (Fig. 113). In this last we have the hammerhead with very decadent Anglian scrolls and plaits of Anglian origin, for they are of common occurrence in the North, though here, as on a cross (Fig. 180) in Hexham

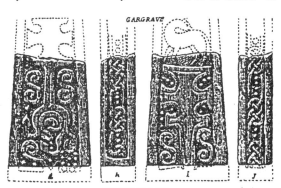

FIGURE III

FIGURE 112

91

church and the Hart and Wolf slab at Lancaster (Fig. 171), turned into Viking Age ornament by adding snake-heads to the strands. On Fig. 113, side *a* is a late crucifix and beneath it a figure with the round shoulders often seen in late tenth century drawing; on one side of him are smith's tools, birds on the other. One must resist the temptation to read Sigurd or Völund into the story; there is not quite enough to justify such an explanation. But it is interesting again to see the last of Anglian art passing into Scottish, with this

FIGURE 114. YORK

13. *Kilmorie*

FIGURE 113

hammerhead that gives one more link between Galloway and Yorkshire.

A few careless and shapeless heads might be collected from very late crosses, free-armed and therefore of Anglian tradition:—Kirby Hill near Aldborough, a little cross over the south door in the porch with seven bosses in the centre circle, equating it with late types at Lancaster (Fig. 128); Londesbrough, a rudely outlined head with stringy plaits; Anthorn on the Solway, the stone no doubt worn and very likely post-Conquest, but once perhaps like the nondescript cross from Wooler (now No. 11 at the Durham Cathedral Library); and for complete departure from precedent, Durham No. XLIX, from Startforth, which has none of the marks of a pre-Norman monument. But also there are a few with the armpits square, such as one with ring-twist at Forcett, another with a figure holding a snake and on the reverse the seven bosses and plaits, at Brigham (Cumberland) and a grave-slab at York (Museum, Hospitium No. 5) which has a cross in relief with the Anglian offset to the head while the arms, expanding slightly,

92

run to angles a little less than right angles at the armpits (Fig 114 *b*). With it was found on the cemetery site at the New Market, York, the square crossed slab (*a*). Now by the leaden cross found at St Austin's Abbey, Canterbury, (and described by the Rev. R. U. Potts, F.S.A., in *Archaeologia Cantiana*, xxxvii, 211) we have at least one safe date for the form of 114*b*; it is to Wlf-maeg, sister of Wlfric the abbot, and states that she died on March 11th, 1063.

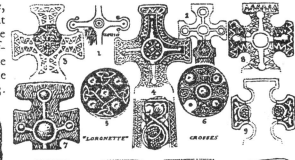

FIGURE 115. YORK

Another date has been suggested by the somewhat similar leaden cross found at Bath in 1898 and read by Mr. Charles E. Davis, F.S.A., as indicating either 972 or 977. It is unfortunate, however, that the lettering is least legible just where the date might be read, and guesses at the identity of the lady Eadgyfu do not help.

FIGURE 116

One more form is worth mentioning as a precaution, that of the so-called Saxon cross at Corbridge, with diagonal grooves meeting near the centre. That is the form (Fig. 115) of a finial from St Crux, York (in the Museum, Hospitium No. 18); of the Cross Lacon at Rheda (Cumberland); St Bees (post-Conquest) 'resting cross' and many more, which can safely be regarded as post-Conquest.

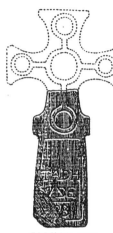

FIGURE 117

On heads of Anglian, free-armed shape, and very rarely on wheel-heads, there is sometimes a device as of a superimposed cross with bosses (now and then only rings) at the ends of the four arms. This we have already called the spine-and-boss or 'lorgnette' from its likeness to a lens with a handle, and it has been suggested (p. 8) that it is a survival of a cut-out cross affixed to the wooden staff-rood (or to any wooden memorial) with nails, of which the heads are represented by the five bosses. Nothing exactly the same occurs in what is called Christian art, but something like it in the well-known disc-heads of bronze pins, in which a plain flat cross has been *appliqué* to the highly ornamented surface. If the earliest Northumbrian grave-monuments were usually of wood — and the fact that wood-work was a speciality of the Northern nations, before they began to carve stone, points that way — then this device is easy to understand. For the sake of giving a number of examples together, Fig. 116 is repeated from a paper by the author in 'The Antiquary', N.S. ix, May 1913.

We have seen the lorgnette clearly in the Lindisfarne slabs (Fig. 16*k*) of which Mr C. R. Peers describes and figures ('Archaeologia' vol. 74, pp. 261ff.) no less than five with this kind of cross, to be distinguished from the normal Clonmacnois type with semicircles (not rings) at the ends of the arms. At Hartlepool one example has been found (Fig. 16*b* and 116-1) and this not exactly the same as those at Lindisfarne; the rings are ornamented with an extra line outside, ending in curls, and the spines, instead of meeting the centre in straight lines, curve away round it in the form of St Cuthbert's pectoral cross. A very neat form is that on the cross (Fig. 116-2 and 117) to Adhusa the priest (York, Hospitium No. 13) which is from Ripon; and at Ripon is the fragment of a head (Fig. 116-3) which bore a lorgnette and chevron.

BRIDEKIRK

FIGURE 118

Northallerton is the place where we have the finest instance of the lorgnette in a tall free-standing Anglian head (Fig. 30 and 116-4) and this is a highly interesting example. The centre (Fig. 116-5) holds five bosses surrounded with an interlacement, almost exactly like that of the centre of the Ormside Cup (Fig. 116-6) while the frame

94

of the cross-head is filled with chevron, all very carefully carved. The chevron connects this with one at Carlisle (Figs. 104 and 116-8) which has chevron, and Anglian scrolls of pure style on the reverse (Fig. 116-9). And at Heysham (Fig. 128) practically the same type is found, with lorgnette and chevron but seven bosses within the ring that forms the centre. We have already noted the Ripon school; here seems to be proof that it was working by the middle of the ninth century and that its craftsmen went out as far as Carlisle on the north-west and as Heysham on the south-west.

The fashion of the lorgnette cross, once started, continued for a long while, flourishing chiefly in north Yorkshire and Cumberland where it died out very late. The hammer-head cross at Carlisle (Fig. 116-7) must have been made in the eleventh century when Carlisle is usually supposed to have been lying waste; but here, as at Hexham, burials were made even then.

On the Cumberland coast at Crosscanonby, part of a small lorgnette cross-head was found in 1880 among the rubble of a 'Norman' wall of the church, the carving roughly hacked; no ornament remains from which it can be dated, but the whole series at that place begins in the tenth century. And now we come to the curious group of West Cumberland crosses, once attributed to the 'British' period, in which the ornament is mainly rude spirals, here and there diversified with badly drawn panels of the 'stopped-plait' type. These, because some of them show lorgnettes, can be got into something like chronological position:—Beckermet St John's (Fig. 116-12) with spirals and stopped plait, debased free-armed form, probably with the hammer-head; Bridekirk, a fragment of a similar cross (Fig. 118 and 116-11); Dearham, the same (Fig. 116-10) but rather

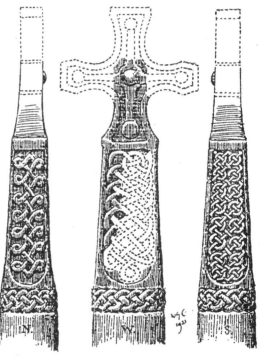

PENRITH GIANT'S GRAVE · THE WESTERN CROSS

FIGURE 119

95

more elaborated, and possibly to be restored with a shaft bearing rude figures formerly interpreted as St Kened of South Wales and his bird, but also showing *swastikas* and so connected with the earlier Norse settlers who probably imported that symbol, elsewhere unknown in monuments of the Anglian type or tradition. Distington and Harrington (Fig. 166) have fragments; and St Bees (Figs. 116-13 and 165) has the latest of the group, with spirals, stopped and freely pelleted plait, and on one edge the clumsy battlement pattern seen also on a late cross at Lastingham, which brings it well into the eleventh century. The head of this St Bees cross was very dwarfed, very debased; it closes a Cumbrian series which we must now consider to begin in the tenth century—a local development, derived from Anglian sources, perhaps distantly from Ripon, but degraded more by the inexperience of the craftsmen than by any long lapse of time.

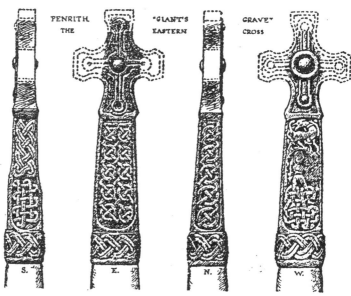

FIGURE 120

The Giant's Grave at Penrith gives two important examples of lorgnette. The cross now at the west end of the group (Fig. 119) is round-shafted and has regular tenth century plaits; see the opening of Chapter XV for the 'Leeds braid' found on its northern side. The cross now east of the group (Fig. 116-16, better drawn in 120) is much later by the gridiron plait on the south and west faces; all earlier interlacings are based on diagonal lines, and this gridiron is found in Northumbria only on very late stones as one at Mirfield (Fig. 216), as well as in Scotland on monuments apparently of the eleventh or twelfth centuries. Probably the earlier cross at the Giant's Grave may be mid tenth century and the later about 1000, for the survival of so many Anglian motives in a district so strongly influenced by Scandinavia warns us against putting it too late. And in passing it may be remarked that this difference in age between the two crosses does away with the old idea that the 'Giant's Grave' is all one monument. It is really a fortuitous collection of gravestones, assembled we know not when, though probably at some medieval enlargement of the church, and further shifted before Dugdale's visit in 1664-5; perhaps once more meddled with at the great rebuilding of the church in 1720-22 ('Cumberland and Westmorland Transactions' for 1923, pp. 115 ff). The arrangement we see now has no significance whatever.

The Kirkby Stephen head (Fig. 109 and 116-18) has been already mentioned; very Anglian in general aspect and linking Penrith to Ripon by its site near the main road over Stainmoor, along which we now retrace our steps to Yorkshire to gather up some late examples. A cross-shaft at Hauxwell (between Catterick and Wensley), which used to be called 'Crux Sancti Jacobi' and attributed to the seventh century James the Deacon (Bede, *Hist. Eccl.* ii, 20), has one remaining boss which pretty certainly is part of this device. The plaits on this shaft are those common to the tenth century and to the transition from pre-Danish Anglian to Anglo-Danish. From Gainford (Fig. 116-20) a little further north, now at Durham (Cathedral Library No. xxxvii) is the neck of a free-armed head with spine-and-boss, and on the shaft a bit of the Scandinavian chain or vertebral pattern which marks it distinctly as of the

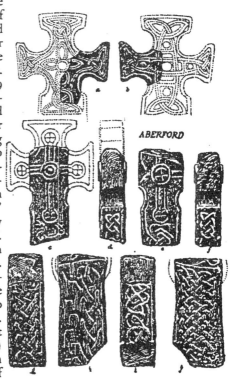

ABERFORD

FIGURE 121

tenth century and of the same transition style. At Gilling West, between Hauxwell and Gainford, are two lorgnette crosses, one (Fig. 13-7) the plain free-armed kind, and

o

the other a rare example of spine-and-boss on a wheel-head. And at Forcett, between Gilling and Gainford, is a very debased specimen (Fig. 116-19) with the lorgnette cross on the shaft or slab, three shapeless pig-like beasts crawling above it and very bad plait below.

Crossing the Vale of Mowbray by way of Northallerton to Cleveland we come to Great Ayton under Rosebery Topping, and find a free-armed head (Fig. 122) bearing a crucifix on one side and a lorgnette on the other. A little north is Stainton-in-Cleveland with a slab or cross-head (Fig. 116-21) with armpits rounded as at Hartlepool (Fig. 16 h); the rings at the arm-ends are marked with crosses, one in relief and the other incised; it has no ornament from which it can be dated. East of this, at Upleatham near Saltburn, is a free-armed head with the lorgnette, a debased plait with a bird or beast on the reverse and a knot on the arm-end, late tenth century or early eleventh. Turning southward, on the great north road, is Aberford where we find another lorgnette on a free-armed head (Fig. 116-22 and 121 *cdef*) the rings at the spine-ends crossed as at Stainton, and fragments of tenth century transition design on the same stone below.

This review seems to make it more fully evident that Ripon was the centre not only of a considerable school of cross-carving but also of the lorgnette motive, adopted after 800 and repeated for a couple of centuries up and down the great north road and across into Cleveland, by Ripon-bred workmen and the heirs of their traditions.

One step further may be taken. The Sinniness (Fig. 116-17) and Craignarget slabs (Fig. 18) bear something like a spine-and-boss form. We have connected these early Norse stones in Galloway with Aspatria in Cumberland and it is conceivable that the Norse colonies on both sides of the Solway had much in common during the tenth century. It is possible that, not being stone-cutters, they got a workman from Cumberland to come over and help them; the trip in a boat is easy, and until the Edwardian wars the Solway united rather than severed its two shores. If that is so, we have run through a long series of curious changes, down a wandering stream of development whose well-head was at Ripon. And incidentally the study helps to check and verify the stages of Northumbrian art in general.

Chapter X. Crucifixes

AFTER looking through the cross-heads we are in a better position to consider the crucifixes, some of which indeed have been mentioned. They are not all on cross-heads, though the lateral arms are the natural place for the extended hands of the figure, and in a sense every cross means a crucifix.

There has been some doubt as to the frequency of this motive in early times, and as to the form in which it was represented. That it was not unknown, on a small scale at least, before the age at which Anglian carving began, and known in the West as well as in the East, seems to be indicated by such examples as are figured by Forrer in his *Reallexicon* (article *Kreuzigung Christi*). He shows, for the seventh century, a Syrian bronze cross with the figure fully draped (p. 428); he attributes to the seventh or sixth, a silver filigree pendant found at the Christian site at Björkö or Birka in Sweden, rudely stylized (p. 428, 877); to the sixth century a nimbed figure in long drapery, between the sun and the moon, from Achmim in Egypt, and a gold brooch in the Rosenberg collection at Karlsruhe with nimbus and full drapery, between the sun and the moon and the two thieves (p. 427); to the fifth or sixth century, the carving on an ivory box in the British Museum, giving the nude figure with loin-cloth, nimbed in classic style (*ibid.*) and earlier perhaps than these is the classic gem in the British Museum, similar to the last but on a T-cross (*ibid.*). The like figure on the door of Sta Sabina in Rome may not be as old as it has been thought; and we need only allude to the well-known caricature of 'Alexamenos praying to his God', attributed to the second century, to suggest that in the earliest Christian times some representation of the Passion was familiar.

From these examples it seems that there were two early types, one fully draped, of which there are examples from the East, and the other nude, following classical tradition in the West. But it is to be admitted that we have not brought forward any crucifix in stone sculpture. For that matter, we have no free-standing cross in stone to quote as the model of the characteristic Northumbrian monument. Nor have we been able to give the provenance of the Hexham Rood, which might solve the question. We can only say that in metal and ivory, on a small scale, the crucifix was generally known; and when Anglian clerics were importing objects of ecclesiastical art, as we know they did, examples from any part of Christendom may have come with the rest. And if those examples were Oriental, it does not follow that Syrian or Armenian workmen also came over, to make the somewhat rude copies which are all that Northumbria can show.

Passing over the Hexham Rood (Fig. 36) we have the Spital shaft (Fig. 37) which can hardly be of any other period than the group of Hexham crosses so closely akin to it, and by our argument (p. 33 *f*) datable to the middle of the eighth century or a little later. Beside the cross here, the spear-bearer (Longinus) and the sponge-bearer are shown; the figure of Christ is nimbed and wears a tunic which does not come down to the knees. The Ruthwell crucifix (Fig. 101), also on the shaft and not on the head of the cross, is difficult to make out owing to the decay of the stone; but it is not certain that the figure is nude to the waist, or whether it has not a tunic, covering the body, with ample gathering up of folds round the loins. Remains of two figures beside the cross and of the nimbus are traceable; sun and moon have been added to the Hexham design, but in general there is much similarity. Both of these, and indeed all the cruci-

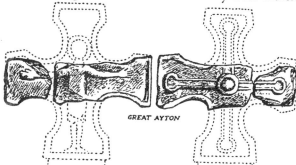

GREAT AYTON

FIGURE 122

fixes we find on our pre-Norman stones, show the feet separated and not crossed, whenever any feet are visible.

After these there is a gap. None of the other fragments of Anglian monuments belonging to the best period shows a crucifix, and no argument can be upheld from the fact. But when we pick up the thread again we find similar motives, as if the tradition had not been forgotten. It is to be noticed that these later figures are very often defaced as if intentionally; the illustrations show the damage; but still we cannot infer that we have lost more crucifixes than in due proportion to other stones.

As Great Ayton is one example with well-drawn hands and arms; the spine-and-boss on the reverse does not date it (Fig. 122). Dewsbury has a shaft-fragment with a

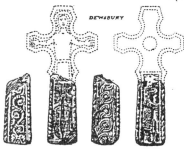

DEWSBURY

FIGURE 123

late Anglian scroll, a plait (Romilly Allen's No. 653) common in the tenth century, and on the front the lower part of a figure, barefooted and with a tunic coming down below the knees (Fig. 123). It can hardly be other than a crucifix of which the upper part filled the cross-head. On the reverse is a curious bear-like creature on its hind legs, holding what at first sight looks like a two-pronged fork; in some lights one seems to see features of a head and a rudely sketched human figure, all on a scale very small for carving. It has been suggested that the mon-

ster was meant for a Manticora or man-eater, as on the shrine-tomb at Meigle and the slab at Murthly, Perthshire, and if so, an emblem of death. Without laying weight on this interpretation we can say at any rate that the stone is a rather early one in the Anglian survival after the Danish invasion, for Dewsbury was one of these surviving sites.

A smaller but perhaps not much later crucifix is seen at Finghall (Wensleydale) on a fan-armed head (Fig. 124). The ground is filled with a couple of *triquetrae* and pellets; the figure nimbed and clothed. The cutting is of the hacked kind that was in use in the Anglian survival and the drawing though conventional is not grotesque. A bit of shaft which, being of the same style and workmanship, may belong to the head, has the double twist which was in use in West Yorkshire (as at Ilkley) long before the better period of the Anglian survival was over.

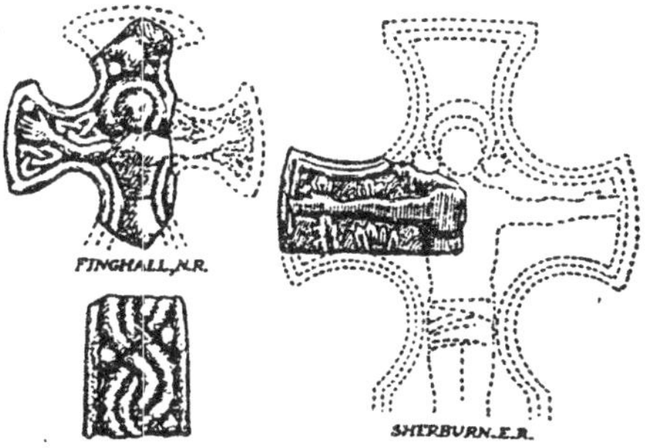

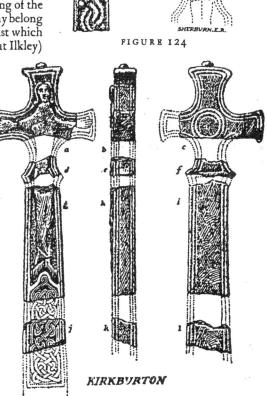

FIGURE 124

Like the Dewsbury stone in being the neck of a cross that must have borne a crucifix head is the fragment from Billingham (Durham Cathedral Library No. xxix). It shows fairly well-drawn feet and legs; on the reverse is the sitting figure of a saint or angel. On one edge is a late bird-form, and on the other a plait of the kind used in the Durham group of stones. Among these, and in the tenth century, we place the cross by Myredah to Eadulf, from Alnmouth (Fig. 79) and the Aycliffe stone (Fig. 97) in both of which the crucifix is on the shaft, and not on the head.

At Durham, among the relics from the foundations of the Norman chapter-house, are two, after 995 when the abbey was founded, but old enough

KIRKBURTON

FIGURE 125

101

to have been considered rubbish soon after 1100 (Cathedral Library Catalogue Nos. XXII, XXIII). They are certainly very ungainly. The Christ is beardless; the tunic comes down to the knees; it has sleeves to the wrists, ribbed in parallel folds like the Jarrow hunter's. We attribute the ugliness of this Durham group to the incompetence of the carver and want of taste in his patrons; it does not of itself mean earlier or later than the Jarrow stone or the Rothbury cross. But the motives show how an Anglian tradition persisted down to the eleventh century.

KIRKDALE

FIGURE 126

At Sherburn, east of Malton, is part of a crucifix (Fig. 124), fairly well modelled and with leaves above and below the arm, which is all that remains. The church, mentioned about 1060, has monuments that seem to go back to somewhat earlier.

Kirkburton, near Huddersfield, has a cross (Fig. 125) which is almost complete though broken into small pieces; very late Anglian, by the plait and the plain back and edges. The crucifix is not well drawn and is very attenuated; it is draped to the feet and has extra folds wrapped around the waist in the same way as at Ruthwell and in our next.

Another tall figure is at Kirkdale, near Helmsley, nude but for an exaggerated loin-cloth, nimbed and bearded (Fig. 126). The shape of the cross-head is that which we have associated with very late work (p. 87).

At Sinnington, not far east of Kirkdale, the crucifix is not badly designed but it is on a head of debased and late form. The figure seems to be fully draped, but the lower part is lost. Under the arms are snakes, perhaps taking the place of the soldiers, for it is not certain that a piece of shaft with the two figures beside the cross-stem belonged to this head. The two figures reappear at Kirklevington on a fragment bearing also the Scandinavian ring-knot (Fig. 127).

At Lancaster we have again a shaft with the two soldiers, made ugly with beasts' heads; and a cross with a crucifix on both front and back (Fig. 128). Each figure has a circle on its breast, filled with pellets.

FIGURE 127

102

This late combination of decorative and representative intentions we see again; but it goes to the furthest extreme in a very odd little cross-head at Wath near Ripon, in which the crucifix is merely hinted by fingers of a hand at the end of the lateral arm.

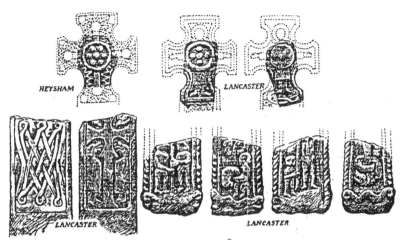

FIGURE 128

Still in the tradition of the Anglian free-armed crosses, but degenerated into the hammer-head, is the Kilmorie slab (Fig. 113). The survival of the leaf-scroll shows its derivation, neither Celtic nor Scandinavian; its grotesqueness is the carver's fault. This appears to date early in the eleventh century; it is likely that very soon afterwards any Anglian tradition would have been lost in that district, which then came under the influence of Argyll and a little later under the Norse of Thorfinn, Earl of Caithness and Orkney. But even under Danish and Norse influence crucifixes were still carved upon crosses.

The first small group we take contains some that are not wheel-crosses, but not ordinary free-armed heads. At Kirklevington on the fringe of Cleveland is a head (Fig. 130) with rolls or cylinders in the armpits; it bears a rude crucifix and on the other side the two soldiers with beast-heads as at Sinnington, Lancaster, and in Fig. 127. A very debased plait shows that this must be of the eleventh century. Then there are two examples of the rudimentary wheel, small in proportion to the cross-arms and unornamented. This type was common at Brompton near Northallerton, and by the random interlacing on the back of the head bearing a crucifix (now at Durham Cathedral Library, No. liv) it must be late, not before the end of the tenth century. The figure here is especially rude, but draped in a full tunic. The other example of this type is at Stanwick, in the head we have fitted to the round-shafted cross (Fig. 13-8) and attributed to the early part of the eleventh century. Here as at Lancaster we see the centre-boss planted on the breast of the figure, which has its thumbs turned up as in the Kilmorie slab.

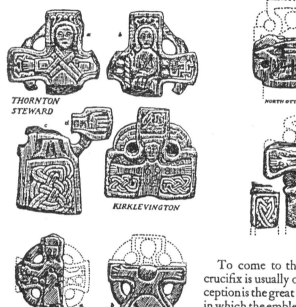

THORNTON STEWARD

KIRKLEVINGTON

THORNTON WATLASS

FIGURE 129

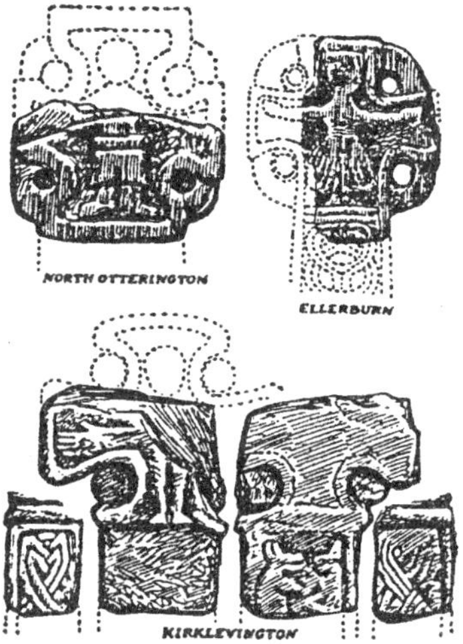

NORTH OTTERINGTON

ELLERBURN

KIRKLEVINGTON

FIGURE 130

To come to the true wheel-heads. The crucifix is usually on the cross-head. The exception is the great Gosforth cross (Fig. 12-2), in which the emblem is unique for Northumbria. The figures are dwarfed and clumsy, but the carving is careful throughout this cross, which is one of the round-shafted 'staff-rood' type and therefore not unconnected with the Northumbrian series.

On the shaft is the figure of Christ (Fig. 184) apparently with moustache and beard, draped in a tunic of which the spread skirt reminds one of Ellerburn (Fig. 130), and with an additional fold or waistbelt distantly resembling Kirkdale. The figure stands free, not nailed upon a cross, within a separate frame of cable (like the angel on the Giant's Thumb, Fig. 162) through which the spear of Longinus pierces and a stream of blood shows that it has done its work. The other person below, with a long plait of hair and a phial-like object, has been interpreted as the Magdalen, 'holding in her hand the Alabastron filled with precious ointment for his burial' (Rev. W. S. Calverley,

'Early Sculptured Crosses' etc., 162); and indeed it is difficult to see what else it can mean.

The remaining wheel-head crucifixes are merely poor work of a decadent age. Thornton Steward and Thornton Watlass in Wensleydale have two each (Fig. 129); North Otterington, a little to the east, has another (Fig. 130) perhaps rather earlier. At Kirklevington, beside the instance already given, is a wheel-head with a step-pattern on the wheel and bad eleventh century knots; the crucifix is so rudely drawn that the hands have no thumbs but only fringes of five equal fingers (Fig. 129). And at Ellerburn near Pickering is the figure (Fig. 130) with outspread skirts, and beneath it a fragment of the Scandinavian chain or vertebral pattern which is so freely used on the Gosforth cross.

We have once more travelled far beyond the limits of the greater Anglian schools to follow the wandering trail of their traditions downhill through bush and briar. At one point, coming off the heights of the earlier style, we have been at fault; there is a scarp and a rock-fall, so to say, which we have had to clamber down; but at a lower level we pick up undeniable traces. From about the close of the ninth century into the eleventh the crucifix was in ordinary use; but by that time figure-drawing had become so neglected that it is no wonder if its efforts have failed to attract notice. For us, however, the stones are documents historical, not art treasures; if we understood all they dumbly try to explain, the dark age of northern England would soon have its story told.

Chapter XI. A Review of the Anglian Period

OF this first pre-Norman age we have now seen examples enough to justify an attempt at generalization. It must be evident that the finer monuments, with better-drawn figures, graceful animals, leaf-scrolls and thoughtfully designed plaits, group together as opposed both to the ruder work which followed it—the dregs of the school—and the work of a different character, done under Danish and Scandinavian influences, which cannot have begun before the Viking settlement. Taking it broadly, Anglian design and carving, in its best state, must have been killed when the country was upset by the Danes; but in certain districts the tradition continued, and even in districts at first ravaged and then settled by the new-comers the older culture revived and flourished, but always with a difference.

We have seen indications of this round about the year 1000, when there was wealth and comparative peace in the north, in spite of occasional and local raids and before the fresh Viking invasions of Svein Forkbeard and Cnút. We know that ecclesiastical life continued in York, also at Chester-le-Street, whence the bishop's seat was transferred in 995 to Durham. Although the age was not marked by brilliant literary performances there are a few works belonging to it, such as the life of St Oswald and the fragment of a Lindisfarne cartulary called the *Historia de S. Cuthberto*, of the time of Cnút. As these are to Bede and Alcuin, so was the art of the Durham crosses, and even the Rothbury cross, to the fine monuments of the earlier age.

Working back, step by step, from the great number of very late relics of Anglian survival, we may arrange the tenth century monuments (excluding Anglo-Danish and Norse) in seven districts.

(1) The north-eastern area, county Durham and Northumberland, has a character of its own. Anglian Northumberland and the influence of Chester-le-Street (900-995) account for the style and for the absence of more marked features of Viking Age ornament seen in central Yorkshire and Cumberland. The plaits we have observed to be often elaborate but always repetitive; they link up with the Scottish series, and indeed there is evidence of Scottish feeling here and there, as in the headstone with a procession of armed men at Lindisfarne (*Archaeologia*, vol. 74, plate lvi), and in the key-patterns, much more freely used than in the south. To an early part of the century we may ascribe the Nunnykirk (Fig. 45) and Falstone (Fig. 44) and, perhaps rather later, the Rothbury (Figs. 94, 95) stones, evidently in touch with Anglian tradition before it was much decayed; but at Hexham the Danish influence prevailed. At York, several destructions of the Minster by fire have left little that marks the survival, though fragments of what must have been fine cross-heads (a beautiful remnant from the city wall, Hospitium No. 11, and that inscribed 'Salve pro meritis, presbyter alme, tuis', No.

12) show that, before the capture by the Danes, York had its share. But the Danes were strong in the capital city, and when we come to that subject we can show remarkable examples of their work.

(2) Ripon seems to have been a great centre of monument-carving. Until the abbey was burnt down by King Eadred (948) something of the old life lingered; and indeed later, if we take Bishop Ealdhun's flight with all his people thither in 995 to mean that it was still a place where they found welcome. And if we have been right in suggesting that the 'lorgnette' was especially a Ripon motive, we can trace the workmen of the belated school up and down the great north road and over Stainmoor, still carrying on their trade.

(3) In south Yorkshire and spreading into the Midlands, we find a tenth to eleventh century style of cross, with Anglian derivation, of which the Conisborough fragment (Fig. 131) may be taken as an example; others are round-shafted, alongside of the Viking Age type. The two coalesce in such instances as Brailsford in Derbyshire, where we have a Viking warrior portrayed on a round shaft (Fig. 14-12). But earlier than that, the Sheffield stone with its realistic figure and late Anglian ornament (Fig. 93) shows that the old school had taken root in the south. Its centre was Bakewell, perhaps not before the fort had been 'commanded to be built' by Eadward the Elder in 924; earlier than that, Dewsbury and Thornhill, out of the Danes' route, no doubt were headquarters of the survival.

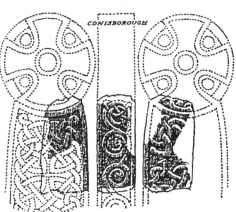

FIGURE 131

(4) Lancaster, by its monuments (Figs. 46, 74), although no trace is found in writing, must have been an abbey of importance and must have survived as such at least until the Norse settlement, which probably began with the second quarter of the tenth century. Further south in Lancashire, as at Whalley (Fig. 132) the monuments are of a later character. The attribution of this and that cross to St Paulinus, who left Northumbria in 633, cannot be seriously upheld. Any tradition to that effect is no more than a tradition of some old antiquary's opinion, dating back to the eighteenth or seventeenth century; make it fifteenth, and we are no nearer firm ground. But at Lancaster and round about was a school derived at first from Hexham and then from Ripon, as its patterns prove, and never touched by the Danes though suffering from the universal decadence of bad times and failing standards. The Halton 'St Peter' and its copy (Fig.

92) may not be late in the age after the Danish conquest, but other works, like the shaft at Lancaster with the beast-headed soldiers at the Cross (Fig. 128), show that the tradition remained until at the same time and at the same place the Viking Age 'Hart and Hound' slab (Fig. 171) was possible.

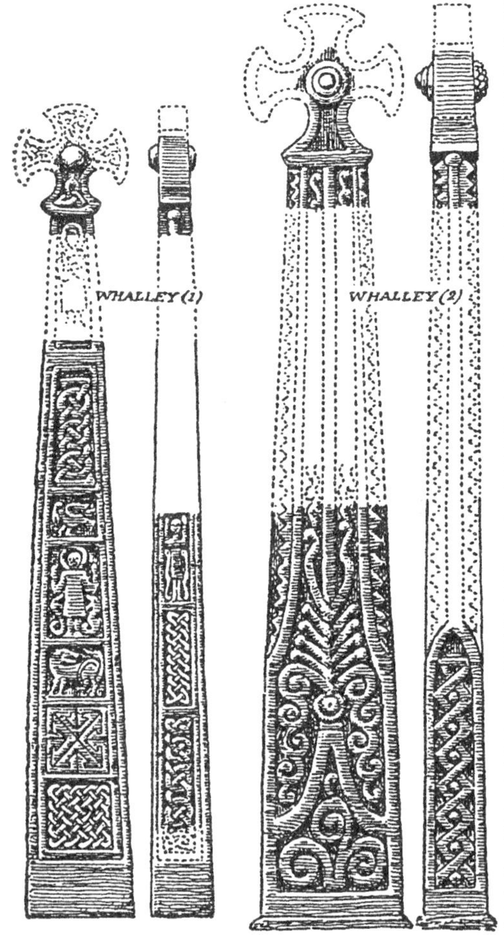

WHALLEY (1)   WHALLEY (2)

FIGURE 132

(5) Cumberland seems to have been fertilized, so to say, by Ripon in the pre-Danish age. Before Half-dan sacked Carlisle, the chevron cross must have stood at the abbey there. Later, though Carlisle was a ruin until the time of William Rufus, its old site must have been hallowed by St Cuthbert's memory, and burials were made there; the witness is in the hammer-head cross (Fig. 116-7). Penrith has its Giant's Grave 'lorgnette' and round-shafted crosses (Figs. 119, 120) apparently contemporary with the 'Giant's Thumb' (Fig. 162), which has a wheel-head along with debased Anglian motives, and the hogbacks are plainly of the Viking Age though one has Anglian scrolls (Fig. 198). Here if anywhere we see the transition, quietly effected; but throughout Cumberland it is no less evident in the leafless Anglian scroll-work which is characteristic of the Cumbrian style.

(6) Whithorn in the later tenth century was practising design learnt from Cumberland work of that 'spiral' kind or, rather, the stopped plait which went with it (Figs. 82 to 85). In the middle of the century a couple of works show Anglian patronage of an Anglo-Cumbrian craftsman (Fig. 80). A little earlier

all the monuments are frankly of Northumbrian character (Figs. 1-6 to 11).

(7) Dumfriesshire, divided from Whithorn by the forest of Kirkcudbright, had its separate attachment to Northumbria—perhaps through Carlisle. Here we find late Anglian monuments, which can hardly be of the pre-Danish period, at Thornhill and Closeburn (Fig. 68); and later crosses, the fan-shaped arms from Glencairn and the fruit-pecking bird from Durrisdeer, running into a definite instance of overlap, Wamphray slab with dragon and leaf-scroll, which speaks Anglian and Norse together just like a bilingual inscription (Fig. 69).

This closes our circuit of the survival sites attributable to the tenth century. Let us look round Northumbria in the ninth century and see what can be found in the way of local schools, late but pre-Danish. We number the areas as before.

(i) In the north-east is very little to attribute to this age. We have the fine slab with bird-scrolls at Jedburgh (Fig. 57), unusually good workmanship but with plaits of a character unknown to the earlier Anglian work; Simonburn cross (Fig. 43), a late effort of the Hexham school; nothing of this class at Lindisfarne; a late leaf-scroll from Jarrow (Durham Cathedral Library, No. XIII) and perhaps the inscribed fragment of a cross-arm now at Newcastle (Blackgate Museum); nothing at Monkwearmouth, where all the decorative carving is later unless we reckon slabs. Hexham shows the cross (Fig. 42) which we tried to reconstruct and placed earlier than 875; from that date the burning of the church stopped any development in a straightforward course.

(ii) Central Yorkshire, on the other hand, is rich in florid and fully matured Anglian, spread over the central Vale of Mowbray, up the western dales as far south as Calderdale, and round about Ryedale to the sea, with an outlier in Holderness. Remembering that we are working backwards, let us take first (a) the stones that we may assign to the period immediately before the Danish invasion. The Hackness cross (Fig. 75) we have found to be of that period; the Patrington stone appears to be as late. The rest are all included in the dales of the West Riding: Ilkley, perhaps a later foundation than Otley and Collingham which are further down Wharfedale; Leeds, where some fragments in the museum imply two shafts and a head of late Anglian, though these fragments contain hardly enough to prove them pre-Danish; Dewsbury, of which the Paulinus cross (Fig. 13-6) and the fragment at the British Museum (Fig. 73) are certainly rather late ninth century; and Thornhill, where everything is either close upon 867 or really a little later, surviving in the non-Danish forest of Elmet.

We come next to (b) the generation before the middle of the ninth century and find a considerable group of delicately cut work with rather florid designs which we have already assigned to a Ripon school:—at Ripon the lorgnette head (Fig. 116-3) and stones built into the buttress of the cathedral; at Cundall the shaft (Fig. 32) probably from Ripon; the Kirby Hill impost, probably from Ripon and re-used in the eleventh century doorway; Tanfield (Fig. 56); the fine Northallerton head (Fig. 30); the Croft stone (Fig. 59), ninth century by its plaits and inverted animals, but showing the delicate cutting of the Ripon school. There is so much of this clever execution in the recumbent Melsonby slabs (Fig. 20), and their animal drawing is so near that of Cundall, that they too must have been carved by Ripon workmen. The same is shown also in the Wycliffe shaft (Fig. 48), the florid shaft and the little slabs at Wensley (Fig. 17 *b*, *c*), and the elaborated plait of the West Witton slab (Fig. 17 *f*). Perhaps too, we may consider the very crisp cutting and far from early motives of the dragon shaft at Otley (Fig. 60) as rather late Ripon work. We may be inclined to go one step further, and remembering the delicate cutting of the monk's head at Otley, on the Angel cross (Fig. 52), we may class this as a precursor of the movement.

That the Ripon products group together impresses itself upon us in proportion as we know the stones; but the date is a matter of inference. No inscription or historical landmark is available. As a class they rank earlier than the period which produced the Ilkley and Dewsbury crosses; they are not the latest which we have to assign to the pre-Danish age. On the other hand we do not yet know the period of the beginnings of Anglian cross-carving; that question we have still to attempt; and meanwhile the Ripon school must be left hanging in the air until we have all the facts before us. We will now look at (c) an earlier class of Yorkshire relics.

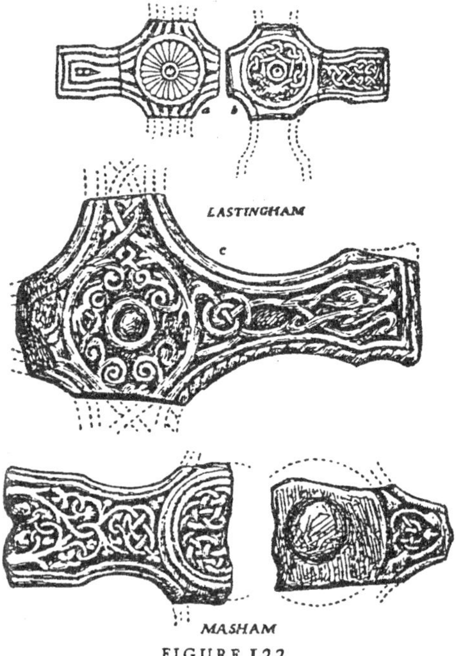

A group of great crosses associates itself with works like the Hexham, Bewcastle and Ruthwell monuments in illustrating the grand style. Everything is on a larger scale than in the miniature Ripon work, and the design accords. Some of the great crosses show a rather more florid kind of scroll than others; the head at Lastingham (Fig. 133c) is of that kind; but at Lastingham are two other cross-heads (Fig. 133 *ab* is one), both pre-Danish and both of later style. At Masham the head which must have once formed part of the great cross (Fig. 13-5) with the round shaft is like the Lastingham head. Both these therefore appear to have been a little later than the fine crosses, not so large, at Otley and Easby; and yet these are not of particularly early type, compared with the much simpler types of ornament in Acca's

LASTINGHAM

c

MASHAM

FIGURE 133

cross, and at Bewcastle and Ruthwell. They seem to be earlier than the Ripon school proper — but again we must leave their date undecided for the present.

(iii) The third area above mentioned was in the south. It contains no relics of the kind we are seeking. Fine Anglian work had not reached the southernmost part of Northumbria before the Danish conquest.

(iv) Lancaster on the other hand had already its church or abbey. Workmen or at least designs borrowed from Hexham and Ripon can be traced in stones at Lancaster, Heysham and Hornby; later at Halton and Heversham.

(v) In Cumberland, Carlisle and Addingham (Fig. 133 *bis*) that is to say the very ancient church swept away by the Eden, from which relics have been brought to the existing church; Dacre (Fig. 58), in Bede's time an abbey; and perhaps Kirkby Stephen (Fig. 109), all on or near the main Stainmoor route, have ninth century monuments. Separated from these by the fells of the Lake district and far away on the west coast are Irton and Waberthwaite, the first with a fine late Anglian cross (Fig. 100), and the second with the fragment of one that may be ninth century or a trifle later (Fig. 134). It is to be remarked of these sites that they stand on the two sides of the great natural harbour of Ravenglass, where the Romans had a fort and possibly in Anglian times there was some shipping; also that the Waberthwaite cross shows some little suggestion of Lancaster influence, and when the sands are remembered as a natural highway rather than a barrier to communications the in-

FIGURE 133 *bis*. ADDINGHAM

fluence of Lancaster is not an idle suggestion. The mention in a twelfth century charter ('St Bees Register', edit. James Wilson, p. 542) of a chapel of St Aldeburga, not a canonized saint though the name is found early in the Durham *Liber Vitae* among 'queens and abbesses', suggests a foundation very long pre-Norman; and the dedication of Irton church to St Paul looks like one that dates from Anglian times.

(vi) Galloway in the ninth century had just lost its Anglian bishop, driven away — it must be inferred — by the great Viking attack of 802 on the Irish Sea and Iona. But Anglian monuments of a style seen in Yorkshire in the ninth century continued to be made at Whithorn (Fig. 6 to 11), which remained ecclesiastically under the archbishops of York thenceforward until the twelfth century.

(vii) And in Dumfriesshire are Hoddam and Ruthwell. At Hoddam we have seen the proofs of Anglian art in tall crosses of the florid type (Fig. 51), and in the 'dolls' house' fragment (Fig. 88) which cannot, by their analogies, be later than the best

III

period of Northumbrian sculpture. How much earlier or how much later are we to place the Ruthwell cross (Fig. 101) and its sister (Fig. 135) the Bewcastle cross? Are they work of the twelfth century?

In the twelfth century, stones of this kind were used as building material; they were out of date. We know what twelfth century ornament was like and we do not see in it scrolls and plaits of the sort we see at Bewcastle and Ruthwell. It may be said that the twelfth century was an antiquarian age, and that revivals of ancient ideals were in vogue, but it is asking a great deal to require that Buethbarn and his brother Addock, sons of Gille-Iosa (Gillēs) son of Bueth, a Celto-Norse family, when they held Bewcastle in the middle of the twelfth century, should have had the means, taste and inclination to spend their money on illustrating a passage in the history of five hundred years before their time; on recording names alien to them in the disused script of a forgotten language; employing antiquarian designers to rediscover tricks of bygone art and to imitate them so perfectly as to match the remains of other great crosses still extant. It is to be noted that at this time the de Vallibus family were not more than the general overlords of the district; and if they were the movers in this enterprise, which is quite as unlikely for them, the memorial cross would have been been set up elsewhere, perhaps at Irthington, when they had their motte and *caput manerii* of Gilsland. Nor were any of the new abbeys in possession of Bewcastle; it was not until the middle of the century that land in the vill of Bewcastle was given to Wetheral priory by Buethbarn, and it is exceedingly unlikely that he gave away the site of his own dwelling, on which the cross stands. Even so, if Wetheral priory had set up the cross, are we not justified in believing that some mention of it would occur in the very full records ('The Register of the Priory of Wetherhal', edit. Chancellor Prescott; Elliot Stock, 1897) which give notices of various crosses on the priory lands but say nothing of this one? All that applies to Bewcastle applies even more to Ruthwell in the twelfth

WABERTHWAITE

FIGURE 134

112

century. Under King David I, who died at Carlisle in 1153, we know that churches and abbeys were built; Mr John Bilson has shown (*Archæologia* vol.73, p.72) how an English mason was employed by the king in Scotland and what his work was like at St Rule's church—the work of the Anglo-Norman overlap, not that of the Ruthwell cross.

Are they then of the tenth century? If that were the date, the designs would be of the period; either a cross somewhat like the fine Anglo-Norse Gosforth cross, or if earlier, one resembling the Rothbury dragonesque style. The tenth century was not a learned age; antiquarian revival at that time cannot be postulated. Both Bewcastle and Ruthwell were in the unquiet condition which must have attended the settlement of Norse-descended incomers, a rude and rough folk, not altogether heathen but with very elementary ideas of Christianity; at any rate wholly foreign to Anglian art and history. And even if King Æthelstan passed by Ruthwell to fight at Brunanburh, which was, as Dr George Neilson showed, Burnswark (and his presence is unlikely because Ruthwell was distinctly out of his route) no suggestion hints that he was ever at Bewcastle, a cul-de-sac at the end of a Roman road which led nowhither except to the fort abandoned in the late third century, or about 650 years earlier. Æthelstan's gifts to Northumbrian churches were munificent; he might have wished to leave a monument of victory at Brunanburh, but Ruthwell would not have been the likely site; and do we know that crosses like these were ever set up

FIGURE 135. BEWCASTLE

to record a military victory? One thing is certain; that neither cross was possible to tenth century carvers. Made then, they would have been made otherwise.

We are pushed back to the pre-Danish age. Some time earlier than 867 but after the beginnings of cross-carving must be the period. So far, we have not been certain of the beginnings, but let us recall the evidences. Up to Bede's death we have found nothing to indicate a tall stone cross; crosses in plenty are mentioned but a staff-rood, or a slab, or the sign of a cross on a rude pillar, or the portable metal, wood or ivory cross or crucifix, satisfy the context in earlier notices. Irish hagiology, written later, and attributing crosses to early saints, is not evidence; no doubt there were crosses, but no tall stone crosses ornamented with carving can be found before 740. Continental and Eastern models for the style are not forthcoming; it seems to be a Northumbrian invention. The first of which we have any reason to say that we have ground for dating it is Acca's. In that we have seen the signs of nascent art; the circumstances which made it possible; the occasion for the effort; the prototype followed in a series that can be deduced from it. Nothing is extant that can be placed earlier, for the Auckland cross, even considered as an early work and by a rival school, cannot be disjoined very far from such things as the Otley 'Angel' cross. If we conceive Acca's cross, shortly after 740, to be the beginning of the whole series; the Hexham school following; the Bewcastle and Ruthwell work a little later, towards the close of the eighth century; the florid style of Lastingham and Masham produced after 800; the Ripon school in the first half of the ninth century and the late Anglian of Ilkley and Dewsbury from the middle of that century—on this theory we have a possible chronology not too short for the development of an active movement in a favourable period, nor so long that one work loses touch with the rest and the momentum of progress is delayed unduly.

It has been hinted already (pp. 25, 26) but in view of misconceptions we risk repeating the reasons why we regard the whole series of Anglian tall crosses as the work of one age and that age a prosperous and cultured period, in which the accumulated wealth and civilization of the seventh century was bearing fruit. It began with King Aldfrith (died 705), the Iona-trained friend of Adamnan and the patron of missionary enterprises in Friesland. His son Osred, though a weakling, had strong support in the ealdorman Berhtfrith, who won a brilliant victory over the Picts, partly regaining the northern realm of Oswiu. The succession was disputed among branches of the family of Ida, but such squabbles between the small bands of personal retainers of the rivals did not mean a general state of warfare. From foreign invasion the country was practically free. Osric (718-729) is doubtfully said to have been son of Alchfrith of the Bewcastle cross, but if he had set up the monument one would expect to find upon it some hint of his relationship to the great name it commemorates. Then followed King Ceolwulf (729-737) of another branch; the man to whom Bede dedicated his *History*; he was at one time dethroned by a palace intrigue but regained his seat and finally retired as a monk to Lindisfarne.

114

His place was taken by his cousin Eadberht (737-758), brother of the great scholar and patron of the arts, Ecgberht archbishop of York (732-766). King Eadberht, says Symeon of Durham, 'overcame all adversaries; and the kings of surrounding countries, of the English, Picts, Britons and Scots, not only kept peace with him but delighted to do him honour; the news of his successes and achievements spread far and wide, reaching even to Pipin king of France, who therefore made friendship with him and sent him many and various royal gifts.' In 750 Eadberht added Kyle to the kingdom of Northumbria and captured Dumbarton, the headquarters of the Britons of Strathclyde; and he, like Ceolwulf, retired to end his days in a monastery leaving his son Oswulf to reign in his stead. But long before the father died, safe in his abbey, the son was murdered by a new rival, Æthelwald, son of Moll (king 759-765), under whom there is no hint of public or political decline of the kingdom at large; and when he was in turn ousted by Alchred (765-774) Northumbria was still in a position to send embassies to Charlemagne, and to take an interest in the conversion of the pagan Saxons. In fact, the Northumbrian Willehad, sent on this mission, founded the bishopric of Bremen; and it is to be pointed out that tottering thrones and distracted populations do not send missions and found sees abroad. The rivalry and the tragedies of the royal houses had little to do with the people in general and still less to do with the church, which continued to flourish under archbishop Ælberht (or Æthelbert, 767-780) the rebuilder of York cathedral on a more magnificent scale. And the clergy were the real rulers of Northumbria.

Then the rival, Æthelred son of Æthelwald, succeeded in driving out Alchred and reigned (774-779), *persona grata* to Charlemagne, who did not like the insecure condition of diplomatic relations, but put his interest upon this branch of the royal line much as Louis XIV backed the Stuarts. Nevertheless Elfwald I soon followed (779-788), 'rex pius et justus', say the chroniclers; in his day St Alchmund, 'eximiae religionis et magnarum vir virtutum', adorned the bishopric of Hexham, dying in 781. The king himself was murdered at Chesters on the Wall and buried, like St Alchmund, at Hexham and equally in odour of sanctity. His son Osred was promptly deposed by Æthelwald, who reigned once more until 796, when he was killed at Corbridge to the indignation of his friend Charlemagne, as Alcuin wrote to King Offa in the letter quoted by William of Malmesbury. It was in his day (793) that the first Viking raid was made upon Northumbria, and Lindisfarne sacked; next year was the attack upon Jarrow and Monkwearmouth; both brief and local mishaps in a country long at peace. And even the Mercian invasion of 798 got no farther than Whalley, where king Eardwulf (796-806, 808-810) beat off the partizans of his rival before they and their allies could enter the heart of the kingdom.

We have sketched the history, dates and all, in order to set down the facts of the eighth century; the recovery of Northumbria and the maintenance of its power, the respect it won from the outside world and the prosperity it enjoyed within its own borders, qualified only by the rivalry of the dynasties which gave it a bad name and led one historian after another to deny it civilization enough to produce the moderate share of art claimed as its output. And if we look at the state of the country in the time we suggested (p. 114) for the Bewcastle and Ruthwell crosses, we find as power behind the throne a series of great archbishops. After Ecgberht, Ælberht, the master of the school at York who was succeeded in that office by Alcuin. Alcuin's poem tells us of the archbishop's magnificent altars and other adornments of the church, rebuilt by Ælberht and consecrated just before his death. It has been thought by Mr George Benson, the York architect and antiquary, that the concrete foundation, discovered in 1829 after the fire, represented the plan of this church; Rivoira attributed it to the earlier church of St Paulinus; in any case the architectural and decorative effort was considerable and the result imposing. After Ælberht followed Eanbald I (780-796) who had taken a great share in planning and beautifying the cathedral. With the men who could execute such a work the making of sculptured crosses becomes much more comprehensible than a hundred years earlier, when St Wilfrid's comparatively modest —though for the time exemplary—church at Hexham was in the building and his masons used Roman sculptures as foundation-stones.

What then becomes of the inscriptions on the Bewcastle cross? Do they not suggest that it was set up in memory of Alchfrith, son of Oswiu, recording also the name of his wife Cyniburg? That may still be true, although it was erected very much later. We have examples of belated memorials. The cross at Dewsbury, however we restore it, on which Leland in Henry VIII's time read 'Paulinus hic praedicavit et celebravit', cannot date earlier than a period about two hundred years after the lifetime of the saint; and we can understand why. Bede (*Hist. Eccl.* ii, 14) said that the stone altar of Paulinus was preserved at a monastery in the forest of Elmet. He gave no name to the place, but if it were Dewsbury (and Dewsbury was no doubt the chief Anglian abbey in Elmet, by the fact of its many relics) the tradition found by Leland becomes credible, and it would be the reason for setting up a great cross—not as a gravestone—but in honour to St Paulinus. Again, the Hackness cross is clearly in honour of an abbess Æthelburga, not asking prayers for her soul as in so many cases but asking her prayers for those who erected it. She may have been the famous abbess of Barking of whom Bede wrote, or Offa's daughter, abbess of Chertsey; but much more likely one of St Hilda's successors at Whitby. We cannot even guess.

Guesses are outside the province of the typologist, and if one is risked now it is only to illustrate a position. We see that, typologically, the Bewcastle cross ought to come into line late in the eighth century. On Michaelmas Day, 792, King Æthelred of Northumbria married another daughter of the great king Offa of Mercia, sister to the abbess. For the second time a Mercian princess became queen in Northumbria. On the first occasion, princess Cyniburg had been married to one whose relations with the Mercians were close and friendly; Alchfrith had converted the royal family, excepting his father-in-law Penda, the stout old heathen who said, 'The man is a nithing who does not stand by his own god.' It is not known how, when, or where Alchfrith, king of Deira, died, but it was after the Synod of Whitby when he took the side of his friend Wilfrid; his widow Cyniburg died a saint long afterwards. And when Offa's daughter Æthelfled (or Ælfled) became queen of Northumbria, it is conceivable that she wished to raise a monument to the royal pair whose fortunes must have interested her. Why at Bewcastle we know not, unless Alchfrid had died there. The reading formerly given to the runes about 'the high sin of his soul' is illusory. So is his death 'under a cloud', for the last we hear of him in Bede (*Hist. Eccl.* iii, 28) is to the effect that when he had sent St Wilfrid to France for ordination as a bishop, his father Oswiu 'following his example' sent St Chad to be ordained bishop of York. But here we have at Bewcastle this fine cross bearing names especially honoured in Mercia. A Mercian princess, with the help of Eanbald, then archbishop and formerly Alcuin's partner in the designing of the new cathedral, would have the means and the motive to set it up.

Giving the cross this date would fit our scheme of chronology if such works began with Acca's, after 740. It would get over one difficulty—the figure of the Falconer, which Professor Albert S. Cook (*op. cit.* 63f) shows to be possible after the middle of the eighth century. The chequers we have seen on a stone from Hexham, pretty certainly earlier. The sundial was in common use in the Roman empire long before; so was the nimbus to various personages, and Christ standing on a dragon had been portrayed on silk in early Christian Egypt (Forrer, 'Reallexicon' pl. 3, 10) if not elsewhere. The plaits are not of an archaic type; they mean some advance in the habit of constructing such designs. And there is one piece of the Hexham motive with all the tokens of matured style, later than Acca's cross, and other scrolls as florid as those of Easby. As to the runes and language, when we find that experts differ, that the subject is intricate and that lapidary material is scanty, we can but say that Messrs. Forbes and Dickins (Burlington Magazine, April, 1914) concluded the period to be eighth century; Professors Baldwin Brown and Blyth Webster ('Arts in Early England', v, 271f) admit some difficulties but believe that there is no need 'for any substantial displacement of the hitherto accredited date', by which they mean about 675. They would, we understand, accept the middle of the eighth century as possible, and they remark that Dr Wilhelm Vietor, who studied the runes in 1895, assigning them to the early period, found no reason in 1915 to change his opinion. The arguments of Professor Albert S. Cook (*op. cit.* 41ff) have been dealt with by Professors Baldwin Brown and Blyth Webster; Professor Cook, however, gives some reasons for regarding the 'Cyniburug' of the stone (not of the photograph) as possible about 800 because of the very great preponderance of the form 'Cyni-' in the earliest part of the Durham *Liber Vitae*. The 'burug' we regard as a quasi-phonetic spelling, like the '-berecht' for *berht* so common in inscriptions. Professor William Peters Reeves ('Modern Language Notes', Baltimore, March, 1920) offers a different reading of the panel -'æft Ælcfrithu El[f]guin [king] eac Oisieu [king]', the 'king' signified by the rune usually meaning 'ng'. He identifies 'Elfguin' with Ælfwine, brother of Alchfrith, and refers the occasion to an early date. And Dr King Hewison ('The Runic Roods of R. and B.', Dumfries, 1921) maintains that the runes on this cross are entirely untrustworthy but gives a highly interesting conspectus of the various readings, from Smith's in 1742 and Howard's in 1801 to an excellent reproduction of their present state. It is amply certain that the earliest antiquaries did not know how to transcribe them. The runes nevertheless were always there, and poor old Maughan, who bears more blame than he deserved, neither invented them nor falsified them. But in this study and in the conclusions here offered we are not trusting to the runes. There is something safer, and that is the typology.

The Ruthwell cross is thought by Professor Baldwin Brown to be earlier than the Bewcastle (*op. cit.* p. 316f). Formerly, but on no very certain grounds, the reverse was supposed by most. It is impossible to believe that they are not by the same group of workmen; their dates must fall within a short period. But while the Bewcastle designers left a panel for inscription, the Ruthwell cross has no such provision; its lettering has been added to the finished work by some cleric who was not content to let the 'pictures' tell their own tale. So considered, a later date for the runes than for the cross is possible; and if the form 'ungget' (facsimile given enlarged in the drawing of the fourth side, Fig. 101) is later than the eighth century (A.S. Cook, *op. cit.* 34) it does not upset our typological argument as to the position of the cross in the Anglian series.

There used to be a tradition that the Ruthwell cross was brought bodily to the place. Bishop Nicolson of Carlisle went to 'Revel' (Ruthwell) for the second time on July 5, 1704, and described the visit in his diary ('Cumberland and Westmorland Ant. Soc. Transactions,' N.S. ii, 195-6). He added that the people said the cross 'was found, letter'd and entire, in a Stone-Quarry on the shore (a good way within ye Seamark) called Rough-Scarr', i.e., at Priestside; it was brought, they said, with a team of four heifers and set up, and a church built over it. What is more, when they got it fixed 'it grew like a Tree, till it touched the Roof of the Church'. Saga-readers will remember how it was reckoned a good omen when a house 'grew' in the building, and this miracle only means that some people find great difficulty in measuring accurately. The stone, however, is of local material; there is no reason for supposing that it came from over the sea or that it was made at Bewcastle. But was it perhaps made at Hoddam?

At Hoddam, five miles from Ruthwell, there was something important in the way of an Anglian abbey, witnessed by fine fragments (Figs. 51, 88), traced back as far as the beginning of the ninth century. Two of the cross-heads are very close to the style of Ruthwell, so close that they must be younger efforts of the same school. Professor Baldwin Brown infers that the missing figure in the Ruthwell cross-centre may have been the Lamb (*op. cit.* 124) and on a later head from Hoddam the Lamb is there.

118

With the fact of such an art centre close at hand we can hardly doubt that the Ruthwell cross is Hoddam work, the first known example and the greatest effort, like Acca's cross at Hexham.

At Lancaster, we observed, the central abbey had daughter-cells at Heysham and Halton. The place called Priestside, from which Ruthwell cross is said to have come, and perhaps also the piece of ninth century interlacing in Ruthwell churchyard (figured with the cross), may have been a cell of Hoddam. At such a cell some great ecclesiastic may have ended his days, and his friends would put up the monument to him there. Some such reason must account for the Otley 'Angel' cross, for Otley was a cell of York; but who were the persons commemorated we know not. It is enough to grasp the connexion which brings this famous work now at Ruthwell within the series of known Anglian monuments, and to remove it from the isolation which it and the Bewcastle cross have enjoyed too long to their detriment.

We find the place of the Ruthwell cross rather late in the eighth century; whether actually earlier or later than Bewcastle matters little. But if Ruthwell is of the Hoddam school, so is also Bewcastle; and the difference between these and the Hexham group is explained.

We might then set out a rough provisional scheme for our whole series of Anglian monuments. Originating from Whithorn with the St Peter stone we have:—

(a) Hexham, beginning with Acca's cross, after 740.

(b) A rival school, creating the Auckland cross, possibly associated with Jarrow and Monkwearmouth.

(c) Hoddam, late in the eighth century, deriving the double scroll from Hexham, but influenced by foreign models or masters. These gave the Roman-classic turn to the sculpture of figures but were not ignorant of such motives as SS. Paul and Antony, ultimately of Eastern origin. In the group we place Ruthwell and Bewcastle.

(d) The carvers of great crosses at Easby and Otley, and perhaps a little later (but still not far from 800) at Lastingham and Masham, and the Hovingham slab and a few minor works.

(e) The Ripon school, beginning—say about 820 or so—with improved technique and slightly decadent design. Among its larger works were the Cundall and Northallerton crosses, the Otley dragons; its delicate carving seen in stones at Hornby, Croft, Melsonby, Wensley, etc., no doubt influencing subsequent efforts over a wide area.

(f) Mid-ninth century, carrying on the general results with later developments in the south-western dales of Yorkshire (as at Ilkley, Leeds, Dewsbury and Thornhill), in the Lancaster district, in Cumberland (as at Irton), and in the north (as at Jedburgh and Simonburn) and the east (Hackness).

(g) And after the Danish invasion, outside the Danish settlements, a survival of these various schools (as detailed above in this chapter) shading off into the Viking Age.

Chapter XII. The Viking Age in Northumbria

FROM the year 867* the great change in the life of Anglian Northumbria began. Pagan Danes invaded the country and put an end to the ancient abbeys which had been the real rulers of the people and the leaders of their civilization. Before looking at the results of this change as seen in monumental art we ought to have before us the course of events, the areas affected by Danish destruction and re-settlement, and the circumstances of subsequent and separate colonization in certain districts by a different race, mainly Norse, from the shores of the Irish Sea.

During the long peace and ease of Northumbria, broken only by faction-fights between small troops of paid retainers, the people at large had grown entirely unwarlike. Even when the great Viking host was creeping northward by way of Lincolnshire they were looking on at the contest of two rivals for the throne, Osberht the 'rightful' king and Ælla the 'upstart'. They had no general military organization which would have ended the domestic dispute; no means of defending York from the aliens who arrived on or about All Saints' Day 867, and took up their quarters in the city. More than a hundred years earlier Bede closed his *History* with these words:—'Our times are so calm and peaceful that many of us, high and low, have given up the use of arms and prefer the tonsure and monastic vows both for themselves and their children; they refuse military discipline. What will be the end of this, the age to come will see.' And in his Epistle to archbishop Ecgberht, written shortly before his death, he recurred to the subject. The end was long in coming, but it came, as Bede anticipated.

Even then they put up a good fight. The two kings joined their forces and stormed the walls of York. They nearly succeeded in driving out the Danes, but Palm Sunday, 868, or the day before, saw them beaten back and their strongest man, king Ælla, slain. During that year the Danes, who had not come to stay but to plunder, left the country to manage its own affairs under a new king, English by his name of Ecgberht, and went south. Ivar the Dane came back in the winter of 869-870 and re-fortified York, but soon after the campaign in East Anglia and the martyrdom of St Edmund, he went to Ireland and died there.

His place was taken by Hálfdan, who tried in vain to subdue Wessex; the battle of Ashdown is dated January 8th, 871, and the young king Ælfred succeeded for the time

---

* The date of the capture of York was probably November 1st, 867, as Roger of Wendover gives All Saints' Day for the move of the Danes from East Anglia to Northumbria. Then the rival kings, Osberht and Ælla, made up their differences 'late in the year' (*Anglo-Saxon Chronicle*), joined forces and attacked the Danes in York. Roger of Howden gives the date of the battle at which 'both kings' (perhaps only Ælla) were slain as 'xi Kal. April, being Saturday before Palm Sunday', within the year 867 which he, according to use in the twelfth century, made to end on March 25, 867-8. The *Historia de S. Cuthberto* makes the Danes arrive at York 'in sancto die Palmarum', but it clear that this was the time of the battle which confirmed them in possession.

in forcing the Vikings back into the Midlands. Thence in 875 Hálfdan turned north. By this there was a new king of Northumbria, Ricsig, of whom we know nothing but that he was not disturbed from whatever position he held while Hálfdan marched through, sacking and burning the abbeys which were his objective because they contained the wealth of the country. Archbishop Wulfhere had retreated to Addingham in Wharfedale (Symeon, *de Archiepiscopis Ebor.*) where he stayed in safety until the storm blew over; he had been deposed by the people for a short time, but soon regained his position. He came back to York in 878, 'after the death of king Ecgberht' —either the original nominee of the Danes or a second of that name.

By that time things were settling down. Hálfdan in 875-6 no doubt sacked the abbeys all up the central vale of Yorkshire and as far as Lindisfarne; he also made a raid over Stainmoor, ruining Carlisle and probably Hoddam, but not Whithorn. He followed the beaten paths, mainly Roman; there was no good track through the wilds of Kirkcudbright. Up the dales of Yorkshire, even the twenty miles from the main road to the refuge of the archbishop, he did not venture. In fact his army cannot have been very numerous; it was well armed and remarkably well drilled, as one sees from the favourite Viking manœuvre of the feigned retreat and rally, which means discipline and attention to the word of command. That it was bold and reckless of suffering even to its own people, every saga-reader knows, and no doubt there were atrocities. But the sting of the invasion, to the cultivated, Christian folk of Northumbria, lay in the fact that they were being trodden under foot by a race they despised. Capable as the Danes were and skilled in the rougher craftsmanship of seafaring and war, they were illiterate, ill-mannered heathen who had no respect for all the conventions that had made the life of Northumbria civil and comfortable to the people at large for two centuries past. The more one learns of their paganism the less one regrets its loss, picturesque as it appears from a distance; and though they had fine arts of their own, the sequel shows that they were unable to adapt themselves to the higher standards long since achieved by the complex-natured Anglo-British Northumbrians. It may be that native culture had gone as far as it would go, and that sooner or later it must fall; but to fall before a ruder race was an unrelieved calamity.

In 876, after ravaging the north, Hálfdan 'apportioned the lands of Northumbria, and they [his followers] thenceforth continued ploughing and tilling them' (Anglo-Saxon Chronicle). In 883 Hálfdan was dead, and Eardwulf, bishop of Lindisfarne, had returned from Whithorn with the relics of St Cuthbert. We then have the romantic story of king Guthred as told 150 years later in the *Historia de S. Cuthberto* to this effect: Abbot Eadred of Carlisle, one of Eardwulf's companions in the pilgrimage, dreamt that St Cuthbert bade him go to the Danish host on the Tyne [by which we understand the 'thing' of the Danish settlers already tilling their newly acquired lands in county Durham] and beg them to join with him in ransoming one Guthred son of Hardacnut [Dane by his name] from the service of a certain widow-lady. Early in the morning the payment was to be made; at noon the ransomed thrall was to be present-ed to the assembly as a candidate for the throne; at three in the afternoon he was to be set on the [thing] mount at 'Oswigedune', a gold bracelet on his right arm, and to be acclaimed king. As soon as he was king the abbot was to ask him to grant all the land between Tyne and Wear to St Cuthbert with right of sanctuary for thirty-seven days to all, even manslayers, who took refuge there. Which was done to the letter, says the legend; and we are free to disbelieve as much as we like of it, except that we cannot doubt the existence of king Guthred (883-894) without throwing overboard a variety of chronicles. Coins however suggest that he was known as king Cnút and that he reigned together with a king Sietred or Sigeferth. And yet, however we regard the story, it fits in with the return of the archbishop to York and the translation of the dio-cese of Lindisfarne to Chester-le-Street (900) as an illustration of the comparatively rapid settling down of the Danes into their new surroundings. Pretty certainly they intermarried with the Angles, and the second generation after 876 grew up as Christ-ians and home-bred Northumbrians by the turn of the century.

The area they occupied at first was the central vale of Yorkshire, with the East Rid-ing and the eastern part of co. Durham. Cleveland, even at the time of Domesday Book, was chiefly forest and moor, and, as the late Canon Atkinson pointed out, its villages then had names mostly Scandinavian, showing that it was unoccupied by the pre-Danish Angles; indeed, the place-names and monuments suggest that its rougher country was not filled up until later, and by Norse colonists. So also with the Western dales and nearly all the West Riding. Later on, when the Danes had further amalga-mated with the English, they or their descendants found their way into these parts, as also sparsely into Northumberland and Cumberland, which at first were left to natives after Hálfdan's raid. For Danish influence on art, therefore, we must look at the main area of Danish settlement, and we shall not be disappointed.

The Norse, or more strictly-speaking, Norse-descended people of Ireland, the Isle of Man, the Hebrides and west coast of Scotland, seem to have begun to settle in the western parts of Northumbria during the tenth century. There are traces of earlier raids in such pagan barrows as have been explored at Aspatria and Hesket-in-the-Forest, Cumberland; their attacks may be inferred from ninth or early tenth century coins found at the ancient stronghold of Castlehead near Grange-over-Sands, where pro-bably the Anglian neighbours took refuge when pirate ships were off the coast. Per-haps also the enormous fibulae found at Fluskew Pike near Penrith and near Casterton (Westmorland) may be pagan relics.* But at an early age in the settlement many colonists must have been Christianized by some generations of life in Ireland or the

* 'Moreover I must not be silent concerning the *torques* called St. Canauc's, like gold ... in four pieces wrought round, joined together artificially, and clefted as it were in the middle, with a dog's head, the teeth standing outward; esteemed by the inhabitants so powerful a relic that no man dares swear falsely when it is laid before him' (Giraldus Cambrensis, 'Itinerary through

isles. We hear of Örlyg of the Hebrides who about this time went to Iceland after learning from a bishop named Patrick to revere St Columba, to whom be actually built a church at Esjuberg (Landnámabók, i, 12) and 'wise men say that some of the settlers in Iceland were christened men, most indeed of those who came from the Hebrides; such as Helgi the Lean, Örlyg the Old, Helgi Bjola, Jörund the Christian, Aud the Deep-minded, Ketil the Fool and others' (*ibid.* v, 15). And when in the west of what was Northumbria we find dedications to SS. Patrick, Bridget, Columba and other distinctively Gaelic names, along with monuments datable to the tenth century, we cannot doubt that they represent foundations of that period by the Norse. The alternative, sometimes advanced, is that they are survivals from missionary visits by saints whose lives we know well enough to be fairly certain that they did not preach in those parts. Indeed, the common idea that all Norse burnt churches at sight is a mistake. Vikings often did so in the ninth century; rarely later, at the time when the Norse settlement of Cumbria was made.

As for the dates of these settlements, we have to start with the story of Igmund or Ingimund who came from Dublin in 900 to find a home in Cheshire ('Three Fragments', 227). The settlement in Cumberland is placed by Professor Ekwall, from philological analysis of place-names, after the first quarter of the tenth century ('Scandinavians and Celts in N.W. England'). In Dumfriesshire, where the evidences are clearly similar to those of Cumberland, the period must be much the same. On Morecambe Bay and in Lancashire it was possibly a little earlier. From the coast they probably pushed up into the Lake district dales, where there was no Anglian population, and the mixture of Gaelic names, as in Iceland, shows whence these people came (for details see the author's 'Lake District History', Wilson, Kendal, 1925, pp. 41 ff). We have named Cleveland, and it is probable that they also penetrated Craven, the western dales of Yorkshire and the forest of Elmet (the author's 'Handbook 2' to the Tolson Museum, Huddersfield, pp. 45 ff). As sheep-farmers, the men who could thrive in Iceland could thrive on the fells and moors of the north, where the Angles had found no land suitable for their corn and cattle. And so, in reviewing the monuments, we have to remember the two distinct races, both basing their monumental art upon the types they found in Northumbria but developing according to their different tastes and powers. In a while they met at York, where Viking rulers, at first Danish by extraction, but later Norse, reigned over the country until the middle of the tenth century. After that, the distinctions began to be effaced by blending, until in the eleventh century there was a tendency to revert to the original Anglian character, but never with the intelligence and charm of the earlier period. That, once lost, was possible no more because the people were no longer the Anglo-Britons who had exhibited it.

Wales', i, 2). Apparently a Norse holy ring or 'Sancta Bega', such as was kept till the thirteenth century at St Bees in Cumberland, and used in Christian times as it had been used by pagans to swear by. Were the great fibulae meant for some such purpose? They are too large for personal wear.

To close this parenthetical chapter it is enough to name the subsequent events we have to bear in mind when we consider the Viking Age in Northumbria.

After Æthelwald, king Ælfred's rebel nephew but elected king of York, was killed in 905, we find in 911 two kings, Ecwils or Eowils, who does not appear on the coins, and Hálfdan II to whom perhaps may be attributed coins which have been supposed to belong to the great Hálfdan. That Eadward the Elder of Wessex was actually for a while ruler of Northumbria is shown by a coin bearing his name along with a York moneyer's. But this 'foreign' domination was closed by the invasion of a Viking from Ireland, Ragnvald (Reginald or Ronald) O'Ivar, who fought a battle at Corbridge (date variously given as 918 or 921) and made himself king at York as the first of a short line of Viking rulers. He was followed by Sigtrygg Gale, also descendant of Ivar, who so far yielded to the circumstances of his position as to turn Christian and marry king Æthelstan's sister. It must be remembered that all the while there were archbishops at York and bishops at Chester-le-Street; the country was Christian, and environment absorbed the adventurer. When Sigtrygg died, Æthelstan would not allow his sons (by a former Irish wife) to succeed. To break the Viking power he marched north and through Cumbria into Scotland, and his fleet ravaged the coast as far as the Norse settlement of Caithness. The reply to this, engineered by Olaf Cuaran, son of Sigtrygg, was the great combination of all the Vikings and their friends, ending in the famous battle of Brunanburh or Burnswark in Dumfriesshire (937). In that combination we do not find Anglo-Danish Northumbrians, though the Norse of Cumbria joined against Æthelstan and shared the defeat.

While Æthelstan lived, none dared to stir; but when his brother Eadmund came to the throne, Olaf Cuaran reappeared (941-944). Eadmund drove him out, and then proceeded to Cumberland, apparently with the purpose of putting an end to the settlement of Vikings in the west. He expelled the last Cumbrian king, Dunnagual (by the Cymric form of his name) or Domhnall (by its Gaelic form), later known as Dumnail or Dunmail, son of Owain, and handed over Cumbria and Strathclyde to Malcolm king of Scots to hold on condition of his allegiance to England. From this we gather that the Norse, north and south of Solway, had multiplied considerably in the past twenty years and were still a threat to the southern English, whose main policy was to defend themselves from the terror of the Vikings. 'A furore Normannorum libera nos, Domine!' was said to be the litany of the age.

Olaf Cuaran being expelled for the time*, another Viking took the throne of York, Eric by name. His identity has been much discussed. It is agreed that he was son of a king Harald, but whether Harald Bluetooth of Denmark or Harald Fairhair of Norway is the question. Up to the time, these kings of York had been of the Danish line,

---

* The dates are uncertain, but the sequence was—Olaf Cuaran, 941-944; Eric for a year or two; Olaf again, and Eric once more, slain perhaps 954 or earlier. The famous Olaf went to Ireland and died at Iona in 981, travestied in legend as Havelock the Dane.

and most of the chroniclers, writing more than two centuries after the events, call this Eric a Dane, because 'Dane' has always been the English name for a Viking just as 'Saxon' has always been the Celtic for Englishman. But Roger of Wendover states that this Eric was slain 'at a lonely place called Steinmor', somewhere in Northumbria; no doubt Stainmoor, the pass on the main road between west and east. This tallies with the tradition preserved by Snorri Sturluson in the *Heimskringla*, who gives a circumstantial account of the battle 'a long way up the land' where Eric 'Bloodaxe', son of the great Norse Harald Fairhair, was killed; and it seems clear that it was he who was the last king of York.

The value of this detail is not negligible. Skene, in an ingenious note ('Celtic Scotland', i, 363) suggests that a great raid by king Malcolm (949, *A. S. Chron.*) when the Scots ravaged the Tees valley and carried off the spoils of the 'Albidosi' or 'Nainndisi', which being interpreted 'na Fhinndisi' means the White people of the Tees, was a raid on the Finn Gall, White Vikings or Norse, as distinct in general Celtic use from Dubh Gall, Black Vikings or Danes. It implies the settlement, perhaps under Eric, which ultimately occupied Cleveland, and gives us a reason for Norse characteristics in the monuments thereabouts.

After 954 Northumbria (excluding Cumbria) became more closely attached to the England of the south. Some interchange of ideas became possible, such as the introduction of tall crosses into the Midlands. And when Svein Forkbeard came in 1013 with his great fleet, the north welcomed him. There was some little resistance at first to king Cnút, but the new Danish rule made no real difference to Northumbria. The Anglo-Danes were a rough and turbulent race; what they tried to do in the way of art we have seen at Durham; times had changed since the eighth century. And then following on the invasion of Harald Hardráda and Tosti, beaten off at Stamford Bridge on September 25, 1066, the final downfall of Northumbria was accomplished when William the Norman in 1069 systematically and ruthlessly ruined the best districts and when in 1070 Malcolm of Scotland swept up the poor leavings.

With the general course of history in mind we are able more readily to understand the monuments of the Viking Age.

Chapter XIII. Anglo-Danish

KINDLY turn once more to the Hackness cross. The lower stone (Fig. 75) bears an Anglian inscription to the abbess Æthelburga; on another side it has part of two beasts with double outlines such as are seen on no beasts on Anglian crosses of the earlier age. And yet these must be pre-Danish because Hackness, as a nunnery, was ruined at the invasion, and this inscription can only have been written by or for the nuns. It is not a case of a later gravestone set in a holy though ruined place. It shows that before the Danes arrived a new style of animal-drawing had set in, the first beginnings of a style which matured later under Danish influence.

THORNHILL
YORKS.
FIGURE 136

Hackness does not stand alone as an example. The 'Ærswith' stone (Fig. 31) though we cannot definitely date it earlier than the Danish settlement, is not a Danish monument; because Collingham, well up Wharfedale, was pretty certainly not in the first Danish colony. Crofton, with its double-outlined 'giraffes' (Fig. 64) was even more out of their way. The ugly cross at Urswick (Fig. 66) was certainly erected before the Vikings settled at the place, and it betrays the new style by a joint-spiral in one of the figures; an incised mark, not a crozier in relief. At Thornhill in Elmet, Eadred's stone (Fig. 136) with its purely Anglian inscription, has animals of the new form though not double-outlined. The fox and grapes at Ilkley (Fig. 49) has on the adjacent side a bird-like creature in the new style; so also even the dragon shaft at Otley (Fig. 60). From Lancaster (in the British Museum) is the cross-head (Fig. 137) inscribed in Anglian runes to Cynibald son of Cuthberect, certainly not very late; but the plait turns into a snake. From Overchurch in the Wirral (in the Grosvenor Museum, Chester) is a small recumbent monument with good Anglian runes '. . . . . Pray for Æthelmund', and on the top is a pair of dragons set tail to tail and interlaced like those on the Otley dragon shaft.

All these suggest what must have already occurred to the reader of page 51—in a word, that before the Anglian period was over, and in districts where the Danes did not settle, where they could have exerted no influence on monumental design, a change had been felt in the spirit of animal-drawing. The foretaste of this change can be dated in the case of the Otley stone at least as far

126

back as the middle of the ninth century. It was very slight at first, but before a quarter of a century had passed it gave the double outline at Hackness, and in another quarter-century the joint spiral at Urswick. Whence and how came the new fashion?

If their version of the new style was learnt by the Danes and Norse from Ireland, as generally believed, there is no real difficulty in admitting that something of the sort could have been learnt in England. We have already mentioned the relations of Northumbria with Ireland (p. 10), and seen that the two countries were by no means in watertight compartments. There could well have been some borrowing by way of the Isle of Man, where Anglian influences are traceable, in the later half of the ninth century when the pure Anglian style was already a little outworn.

'Jellinge' is the name given to the style shown in finds at that place in Denmark, dated from about 930 onwards; the style in which long and reptile-like animals, drawn with double outline and curling among the twists of their own tails and tongues (and usually ears) became the principal motive. It is not to our present purpose to follow it back to origins, but only to note that Dr Bröndsted in his valuable work on 'Early English Ornament' (see also Dr Haakon Shetelig, 'Préhistoire de la Norvège,' 1926, p. 349) points out an early stage in finds at Borre (Norway) dated to about 850 or a little later. The style, if this be so, was in the air before the Danish invasion of Northumbria. It reached its climax in the first half of the tenth century and during

FIGURE 137

the second half ran its course, to be supplanted about 1000 by a fresh movement. It is seen in full bloom in a number of English monuments, so distinctly that they cannot but be Anglo-Danish or Anglo-Norse; that is to say Anglian in the fact of being stone crosses, which had not been made by the Vikings before they took the hint in the country of their adoption, but Danish or Norse in the fact of their being ornamented in the imported style. Some stones, however, betray an overlap which shows the transition from work wholly Anglian to work in which native tradition was gradually more and more forgotten, not necessarily by lapse of time but by foreign influence. Dr Bröndsted, in dealing with this period (pp. 187-240), takes a number of monuments showing animal forms, and equates them with similar forms in Denmark and Scandinavia, by which he suggests their date. He distinguishes three groups —the frankly Scandinavian (hereinafter marked *a*), those less so (*b*) and some in

127

which there is only a general reflex of the foreign influence (*c*); and as his classification is of great importance to our study we take leave to state the general result:—

About 875, Collingham (Fig. 31), one side *a*, the rest Anglian.

End of ninth century, Ellerburn cross-head (Fig. 138); Middleton shaft in the tower (Fig. 139); Nunnington cross-fragment (Fig. 139)—all *a*.* Gloucester shaft and Crofton 'giraffes',—both *c*.

Early tenth century, Folkton (shaft at York, Fig. 140 *a*, *d*) and the St Vedast's stone at Norwich,—both *c*.

ELLERBURN

FIGURE 138

MIDDLETON   NUNNINGTON

FIGURE 139

Before 950, Plumbland, fragment of hogback (Fig. 141 *a*) matching early finds at Jellinge.

Round about 950, Pickhill hogback (Fig. 141, *b*), *b*; Nunburnholme shaft (Fig. 152) and three stones from St Alkmund's, Derby,—all *c*.

* 'The new Pickering stone . . . later than the three fragments just mentioned, perhaps from the beginning of X' (Bröndsted, p. 225); whence we infer Ellerburn, Middleton and Nunnington to be assigned to the end of the ninth century.

Tenth century, closer dating undecided, Crosscanonby (Fig. 142) and Folkton fragments in the church, — c.

About 950-975, Gilling, the shaft with offset (Fig. 143); Pickering (*ibid.*), Sinnington two fragments (*ibid.*); Levisham slab (Fig. 26), — all of which match the later Jellinge finds and are classed *a*. York, the Clifford Street stone (Fig. 144) and St Denis coped slab (Fig. 25)—both *b*. Hickling (Notts.) the coped slab; Gainford, two fragments (Durham Cath. Lib. xxxi, xxxii) and Stanwick round shaft (Fig. 13-8) — *c*.

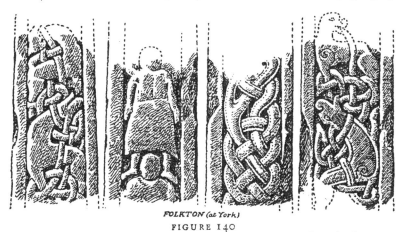

FOLKTON (at York)

FIGURE 140

The importance of this contribution will readily be recognized. In the first place we point out that all the examples come from areas of Danish settlement, or in the case of Plumbland, Crosscanonby and Gainford of Norse, excepting Collingham, Crofton and Gloucester. Collingham and Crofton we have just discussed. Gloucester in the late ninth century as a Viking resort is possible, though Guthorm's army left in 878; but it shows great promptitude if they had already learnt to imitate the English type of monument. Ellerburn, Middleton and Nunnington, as very early in the list, will need consideration when we know what can be learnt (see p. 140) of the free wheel-head.

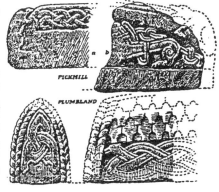

PICKHILL

PLUMBLAND

FIGURE 141

But these animal designs do not nearly exhaust the list of stones to be attributed to the Danish period, nor do we propose mentioning every fragment. A few may be taken as types, and first as to the transition in the matter of scrolls and plaits.

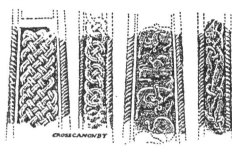

FIGURE 142

Just as the Collingham 'Ærswith' stone is the bilingual inscription, so to say, for Anglian-Jellinge, so the stone found by Mr George Benson at St Mary Bishophill junior, York, is for the scroll. Here (Fig. 145) we see the vine withering away. Its leaves are few and have almost become the snake-head terminations to tenth century strap-work. Its berry-bunches have fallen to pieces and are represented by scattered pellets—the origin of the pelleted

FIGURE 143

plait. On another side of the stone, a mere basket-plait—which is the easy, late way of surface-covering—is broken by a tight volute, resembling the separate little snake at Crathorne and Hexham. This stone shows the manner in which snake-slings of the tenth century, and Viking Age plaits in general, developed in England out of regular Anglian.

At York we expect Danish relics, but several destructions by fire and much rebuilding have diminished their number. Those

FIGURE 144

130

that remain are very interesting. First, the shaft from St Peter's (Fig. 146) with Anglian beasts beginning to be modified in the direction of Jellinge, together with late scrolls and plaits, one of which is the knitting-stitch found also at Leven in the East Riding and at Ingleby Arncliffe (as also on the Croydon Anglo-Saxon bucket); this stone evidently was made before Jellinge became the fashion. Then a hogback from St Mary Bishophill junior, with late Anglian scroll and regular plait; also pre-Jellinge.

Then the very remarkable shaft (from the same church) of the two gentlemen with bugle and hunting-knife (Fig. 147), a late Anglian double-scroll on one side, a quasi-Jellinge panel on the other. St Mary Castlegate, in addition to the dedication stone which records that [Ef]rard and Grim and Æse founded the 'mynster' to Christ, St Mary, St Martin, St Cuthbert and all saints (the later part, perhaps with the date, mutilated) contributes a very neat tenth century cross-head (Hospitium No. 23) and a most elaborate wheel-head of which we attempt a restoration (Fig. 148). On the remaining arm is a little beast, modelled in the round. It is just possible that the four figures were the symbols of the evangelists as elsewhere on cross-arms (at Otley and Hexham) but the nearest analogy is that of the Bilton wheel-head (Fig. 149) in which four little men in high relief take these places; whether they were meant for evangelists, and grotesque merely from want of figure-drawing, is difficult to say. To complete York relics of this age we have the coped slab from St Denis and the Clifford Street stone already shown.

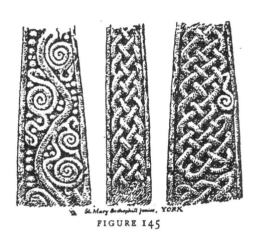

St. Mary Bishophill Junior, YORK

FIGURE 145

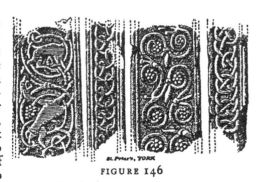

St. Peter's, YORK

FIGURE 146

Let us look round the Danish parts of Yorkshire, going first up the Vale of Mowbray. North of Bilton is Pickhill, where we have seen a quasi-Jellinge hogback; there is also another, with a bear on the end and a regular plait of rather early character. At

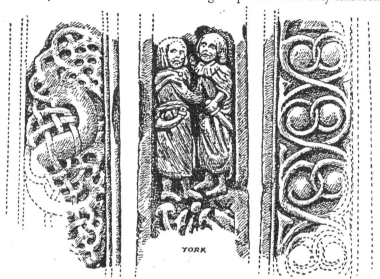

YORK

FIGURE 147

Northallerton among relics of various ages is one cross-head with rings in the plait. Gilling we have noticed; the shaft with the offset and triangles beneath (Fig. 143) ranks with late tenth century analogies in general form; its double ring is of that

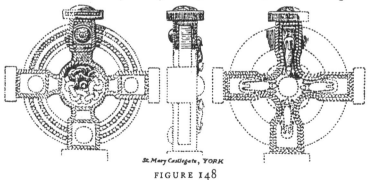

St. Mary Castlegate, YORK

FIGURE 148

period, though not the same as the Scandinavian knot seen often in the Norse parts of the country, and its dragon is no doubt correctly dated above by Dr Bröndsted. The other shaft is round below and has later ornament (Fig. 13-7). It is doubtful whether we have not now travelled out of the purely Danish region into that occupied by Norse; north of the Tees very few traces of Danish style are to be found, and these are

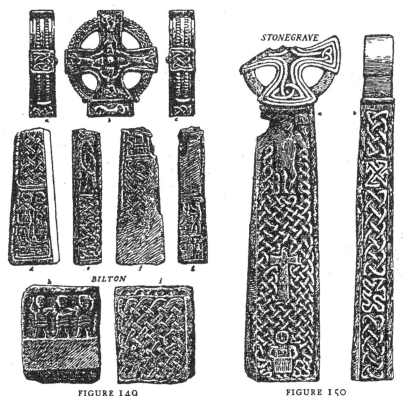

FIGURE 149   FIGURE 150

only the reflex of Jellinge on monuments mainly Anglian, as at Aycliffe and St Oswald's, Durham, late tenth century.

In Cleveland we find only one piece of quasi-Jellinge among the many stones of Anglo-Norse aspect at Easington: and we turn south to Ryedale. Here we have a great group of Jellinge at Sinnington, Middleton, Pickering, Levisham, Ellerburn, Nunnington and Folkton. At Sherburn and at Kirkdale are late stones with buckle-knots of

133

the eleventh century, and eleventh century fragments at Lastingham. Helmsley and Oswaldkirk have hogbacks, the first very rude (Fig. 54*b*) and the second interesting for a figure that looks like a standing Madonna with the Baby in her arms. Two pieces in this district seem to be intrusions—the bit of Norse vertebral pattern at Kirkby Moorside and the most remarkable Stonegrave cross (Fig. 150) with its very open wheel, intricate basket-plait, panels of poor key-pattern and two figures. The uppermost figure seems to be sitting and holding up a book; a rude *Majestas*. The lower one is like the Celtic figures of ecclesiastics wearing a book-satchel round the neck. It suggests that someone from the Orkneys lay buried here, someone later than Eric Bloodaxe, by the type; but in this we have travelled long past the time of the Danish settlement.

NORTH FRODINGHAM

FIGURE 151

Southwards there is a fragment of early hogback at Crambe, with Anglian scroll-work. Then we enter the East Riding and find a wheel-head at Little Driffield and a very rude hogback at Barmston. The North Frodingham cross-head (Fig. 151) is one of the prettiest and most curious of all these Anglo-Danish remains; there are the birds on one side and the beasts on the other, with tenth century T.J.T round the wheel but a rather disintegrated kind of plait-work with bifurcation, indicating lateness. It is interesting to see how late, even in a very Danish district, the Anglian bird and berry-bunch survived, to colour the obviously Danish character of the whole.

At Leven is the shaft connected by its knitting-stitch with the beginnings of Anglo-Danish style in York; on another side, nearly effaced by the mason's scabbling, was a panel of apparently Jellinge character. Of the Nunburnholme shaft (Fig. 152) Dr Bröndsted (*op. cit.* 232) says that the warrior's sword has a hilt of Scandinavian type now dated to the middle of the tenth century and he 'cannot, therefore, follow Collingwood, who dates the cross to the first quarter of XI'. But here, again, we have something not in line with the usual development of Anglo-Danish art-history. The book-satchels on three of the figures look like Scottish types, as at Stonegrave. The general form and disposition of the arches recalls the 'Sigurd' shaft at Halton near Lancaster (Fig. 191) and the arched shafts at Ilam and Checkley (Staffs.). All this group of rather big and elaborate work, based on Anglian survival, which we saw at Durham could linger into the eleventh century, looks like the revival of masonry begun under King Eadgar (959–975) and archbishop Oswald (961-992). The hands holding the arches are of course not the 'gripping-beasts' of Scandinavia, a style long since dead; but they are foreign to Northumbria. The female centaur and baby—odd parody of the Madonna just above —reminds one of a centaur at Tynemouth on a stone which is surely later than mid-tenth century, by its wavy lines framing the standing figure on the adjacent side of the shaft. Some little doubt of the comparative earliness of this Nunburnholme effort must be forgiven, and there is no flippancy intended in the suggestion that the warrior's sword may have been already old-fashioned at the time when it was portrayed. Many a hero of the sagas preferred an ancient weapon. But this curious monument, we confess, needs further explanation.

FIGURE 152. NUNBURNHOLME

South of the Humber lay much Danish territory, but away from the centre of monumental art the instances are both fewer and later. At Crowle is an interlaced shaft with runes on a ribbon, perhaps '—sunr' (somebody's son) : the figures and horseman are clumsy, and its plaits have the character of late tenth century crosses. In Lincolnshire we also mention Colsterworth with Anglian survival patterns, and Bassingham with ring-twist and incised chevron border; both no doubt of the Danish age but

135

without distinct marks of Jellinge influence. On the other hand Northamptonshire, where Christian teaching from Northumbria first took root in Mercia, was already well furnished with examples of Anglian monuments and in this age naturally followed on with more in the new style. At Moulton and Desborough we find quasi-Jellinge animals. At Norwich the St Vedast's stone has been remarked, and at Derby the St Alkmund's; there is also at Hope a late Anglian stone with a beast somewhat in Danish style; and among the many pre-Norman fragments at Bakewell church there seem to be some traces of the same.

Westward and north of this, however, we begin to lose touch with remains that can be said to be rather Danish than Scandinavian. In many places which it would be the province of a *Corpus* to name, but cannot be visited on our hasty tour, there are pieces of the late and simple plait that means monuments of this age. But if we draw a line through Yorkshire a little west of the old North road, turn back at the Tees and run the line through Brompton and Osmotherley eastward to the sea, we shall have enclosed all the remains that more certainly indicate Danish influence. Outside that line, west and north, its traces are very faint, though we have evidences, frequent and fairly consistent, of a kindred style differing a little in spirit and in certain motives, and spreading to the Solway and beyond. And we have already seen that these western and northern parts were brought, during the tenth century, under the influence of the Norse. But the general inference we draw from this review is that Anglian design began to change before the Danish and Norse settlements, and that this late Anglian style led, rather than followed, the developments of art in the Viking Age.

XIV. The Free Wheel-Head

ONE characteristic shared by both Danish and Norse districts, and distinguishing the Viking Age crosses from the Anglian, is the wheel-head. Popular classification sets this down as Celtic, and on slabs, as a form shown in relief, it is common in all the Celtic countries. But as the head of a tall, free-standing monument, cut out in silhouette to show its form against the sky, it is singularly unusual in the Celtic area until the late period of the great Irish and western Scottish crosses.

We have noticed the form on slabs at Clonmacnois, not easy to date. We are warned against certainty as to 'Cuindles' (Fig. 16a) which may not mean the abbot who died in 720. At Iona there are unornamented wheel-cross slabs to Eogan, to Fland and Cand, and to Gilian, on internal evidence undatable, but probably of the period after the rebuilding in stone of the abbey under abbot Diarmaid (814-831), for there is no evidence that stone-cutting was practised there in the early Columban age. In the Isle of Man are many wheel-cross slabs ranging from rudely chipped, badly drawn hints of the Chi-Rho monogram to skilfully executed carvings (see Mr P. M. C. Kermode's 'Manx Crosses', plate vii, 9, 10; plates ix, xi, xii); but as we have it on Dr Haakon Shetelig's authority ('Saga-book of the Viking Society', 1925, p. 19) that the fully developed and ornamented wheel-cross slabs by Gaut Bjarnarson date from about 930 onwards, we infer that the ninth century knew the type in its early stages.

Arguing *a priori* we might conclude that it arose from the Galloway Chrismon imported into the Isle of Man as shown in Maughold slabs. One of these has a pure Anglian cross in a double ring and [Alpha and] Omega; two are inscribed to Blagkimon with Anglian runes. One, inscribed in lettering like that of the St Peter stone at Whithorn '[xros?]NEIT S[ancti]P[res]B[yteri] & EP[isco]P[i] DEI', betrays its origin by the little tail to the upper cross-arm, making it the Chi-Rho. And then we might note how easy it would be to improve some of the deckle-edged slabs (as on plates xi and xii) by trimming the background away from the outline of the wheel-cross, leaving the silhouette (as on plate xiii) and at once producing the free wheel-head. This would have been done in the course of the ninth century; by the tenth the wheel-head would be, so to say, a manufactured article, ready for export.

A priori, however, is not sufficient. Have we any better reason for fixing upon the Isle of Man as the birthplace of the wheel-cross? We have the map (Fig. 153) which means the sum of all the facts we know. The map tells us that free wheel-heads stand thickest in the Island, and next thickest along the opposite coast of Cumberland. Thence we can follow them along the two main routes into Yorkshire, by Penrith and Kirkby Stephen over Stainmoor to Gilling, Cleveland, Ryedale, York and beyond, and by Urswick and Gargrave through Craven and the West Riding. Most of the wheel-crosses along these routes and in Yorkshire are of the tenth century by their associated ornament, none earlier. A third group begins on the coast of North Wales and Cheshire, likewise within easy reach of the Isle of Man; and with later forms, eleventh century, they run south-eastward—not by Watling Street but by ancient roads more or less parallel to it—through to Cambridgeshire and Norfolk. A fourth group is found in South Wales; its earlier forms, late tenth century, start at St Davids, and end with eleventh century examples in Glamorgan. The fifth group is in Cornwall where a few may be of the late tenth but most are of the eleventh (judging by the debased scrolls, which are obviously derived from Northumbria) and some are certainly post-Conquest. The sixth series, running north to Scotland, includes very few examples of the true free wheel-head. One is at Hoddam, late tenth or eleventh century (Fig. 154); one at Lesmahagow, perhaps a little earlier; one at Barochan, with the Gaelic shape of the head, and another at St Vigean's, with Celtic re-entrant volute and key-pattern; St Martin's cross at Iona and the Kildalton cross in Islay are admittedly later. And the seventh group is formed by the twelfth century Irish crosses.

FIGURE 153

Now from the map it is evident that the dispersion of the wheel-head* radiates from the Isle of Man, where the examples seem to be early, to more distant places where we find late developments such as the elaborate crosses of York and Stonegrave, Iona and

* Reference may be made to a paper on this subject in the 'Yorkshire Archaeological Journal', vol. 28, 1925, discussing the examples in further detail. The Hoddam wheel-head has been observed since the map was drawn.

Islay, or the debased ornament of South Wales and Cornwall, or else the mere head-stones of the eastern Midlands. It is evident moreover that the lines along which the fashion travelled were the lines of communication by sea and land from a centre well-known to be head-quarters of the Vikings to regions in which they had interests. The especial motive in the first half of the tenth century was travel between York and Ireland, when the kings of Northumbria were alternately kings in both places; and when once the various settlements had been made there was no doubt a good deal of ordinary traffic among the kindred colonies. They did not live by fighting: your hardy Norseman was primarily a sheep-farmer, next a 'chapman', and only on occasion the bold buccaneer. So if the map tells the truth, we must consider the free wheel-head as sign and token of the British-Scandinavian grave-monument, originated by the Manx Norse, accepted early in the tenth century by the Danish settlers of Northumbria and remaining with the mixed race in their various homes, English, Scottish, Welsh and Cornish.

To go a little closer into the details; we find two main types of wheel-head; and

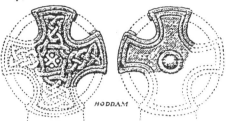

HODDAM

FIGURE 154

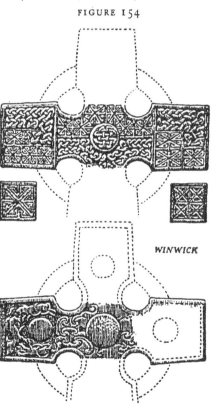

WINWICK

FIGURE 155

139

two or three further varieties, beside the unusual examples already mentioned.

A wheel can be added to the old Anglian cross, with open and rounded armpits; or to the type usually called Celtic, having armpits small in proportion to the block forming the ends of the arms; or again to that Celtic form which has no curves in the armpits at all, but salient angles. This last kind of wheel-head is seen in South Wales, with very debased ornament; pretty certainly late eleventh century at the earliest. The second kind, with four small holes and large arm-ends, shows its most remarkable example in England in the Winwick (Lancs.) fragment with key-pattern and late Celtic volutes (Fig. 155). In this instance it is intrusive and probably late; the repetition of Stafford knots with angles in the strap, and their disposition, crawling round the cross-centre, is unlike anything in ordinary Anglo-Danish or Anglo-Norse attributable to the tenth century, and it suggests an importation from Scotland in the eleventh century. The three figures at one end of the arms may mean the martyrdom of St James the Less, whose attribute is sometimes the saw, or St Simon, the second century bishop; at any rate it is not a memorial of king Oswald, whose last battle used to be located here, but without sufficient reason. The figure at the other end is carrying two buckets—or possibly bells, in which case, why two? But the drawing of these ugly soldiers is not unlike such as we see on a cross-shaft at Lancaster (Fig. 128) and Kirklevington (Fig. 127), probably early eleventh century. Therefore when we find somewhat similar forms of wheel-cross at Ellerburn and Kirklevington we are tempted to place them rather late than early in the tenth century; at a time when Celtic-Viking influences may be presumed in north-east Yorkshire. It may be noted also that the Manx crosses showing decidedly Celtic shape are classed by Dr Shetelig as of the later school of Gaut, who himself used the Northumbrian form we describe next.

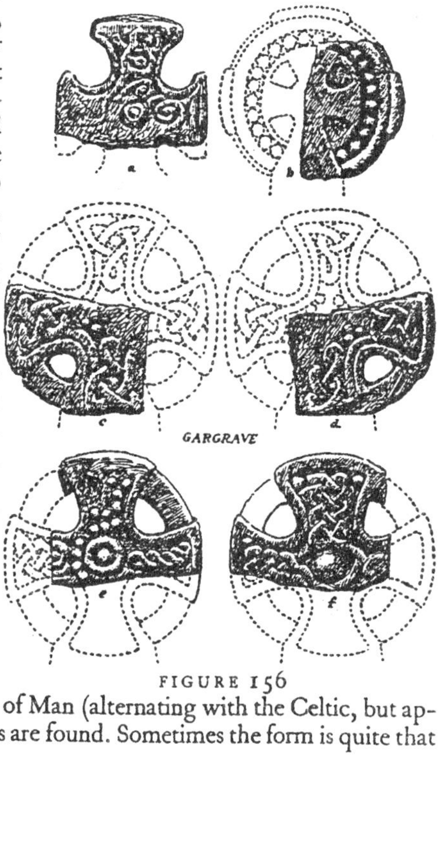

GARGRAVE

FIGURE 156

The type of wheel-head based on the Anglian cross is common both in the Isle of Man (alternating with the Celtic, but apparently early) and wherever wheel-heads are found. Sometimes the form is quite that of St Cuthbert's pectoral with the wheel added; sometimes that of his 'coffin' cross; but always with fairly wide-curved armpits. This is seen not only in Yorkshire, where

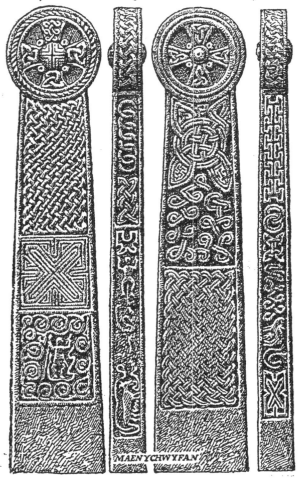

MAEN YCHW YFAN

FIGURE 157

it is frequent, as at Gargrave in Craven (Fig. 156), but always in Cumberland and Westmorland, in Wales (in the older wheel-heads) and Cornwall, and in the late headstones of the Midlands. As time advances a tendency is seen to sharpen the armpits into a re-entrant angle and we have noticed that just before the Norman Conquest we have

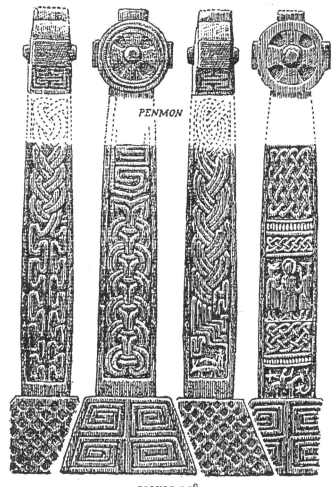

PENMON

FIGURE 158

an example from Canterbury of the plain rectilinear arm. This is valuable if it can be taken to suggest a late date, for example, in the case of one of the Gosforth (Cumbd.)

142

wheel-heads which otherwise resembles the head of the standing cross; and other instances occur at York (Hospitium No. 23 from St Mary Castlegate), and in crucifix heads at Ellerburn, Thornton Steward and Thornton Watlass (Figs. 129, 130), which on other grounds we class eleventh century.

Without much doubt then the normal earlier wheel-head is the one with full round armpits; the wheel-head with four small holes appears to be usually later; with very extended wheel, as at Stonegrave or Bilton (Figs. 149, 150) —and still more at Kildalton (Islay) —it is likely to be later still. And when we find, as we do once at Brompton near Northallerton, that the centre so encroaches on the hole as to give a kind of oblong shape to it, we have either a freak, or something like a well-known type of post-Conquest wheel-head.

Two or three varieties were to be noticed. One has been hinted earlier (page 82) in connexion with the little bosses on the armpits of St Cuthbert's pectoral. These bosses are found on the monuments from St John's and on a head from West Kirby at the Grosvenor Museum, Chester; also on the Maenychwyfan (Fig. 157) in Flintshire. They must represent the local school or individual taste of a carver who lived roughly speaking about 1000, for the ornament of the cross in question is obviously decadent.

Another form which suggests an individual fancy is what may be called the eared wheel-head. Like the last type, but unlike the generality of such heads, these have the wheel overlying the cross-arms, not interrupted by them. The cross-arms re-appear beyond the wheel as little and apparently unmeaning offsets. Of this form there are examples at Gargrave in Craven (Fig. 156b), Diserth in Flintshire and Penmon in Anglesey (Fig. 158); the Chester, West Kirby and Bromborough heads are so designed; and the heads of very well-preserved monuments at Dearham (Fig. 185) and Rockcliff (Cumberland) are the only northern instances we can give. At Bromfield in Cumberland there is a stone almost exactly like the

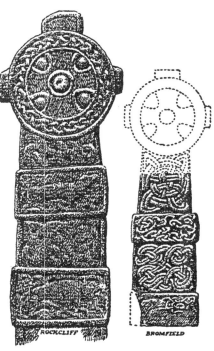

FIGURE 159

143

Rockcliff shaft but its head is missing; both these (Fig. 159) are remarkable for their offsets, and both bear a debased kind of Jellinge beast which brings them down to the end of the tenth century. It may be a fanciful suggestion, but as we have every reason to believe that cross-carvers travelled in their vocation, such a series—all by their ornament much of the same period—may perhaps imply a late tenth century carver who worked in Cumberland, going also to Craven and thence to Anglesey, where he made cross-heads in his peculiar style. Then perhaps he settled at Chester and he or his pupil invented the head which has in addition the armpit bosses that reappear, *minus* the ears, in the Maenychwyfan. And finally the type was imitated in the late cross at Diserth, which like some Cornish heads has the holes cusped in the form of trefoils, and can hardly be earlier than the thirteenth century.

BROMPTON

FIGURE 160

MIDDLETON

FIGURE 161

Two other variants on the wheel-head have been noticed in the course of our study. One has a kind of rudimentary wheel, small in proportion to the head and not pierced or even pitted. Examples are at Durham, Brompton (Fig. 160), Northallerton, Kirkby-in-Cleveland, Kirklevington, Stanwick and Kirkby Stephen; that is to say, it was a fashion local to the Norse settlement on Tees-side and across Stainmoor into Westmorland. The date seems to lie between the tenth and eleventh centuries.

The other is the insertion of a small cylinder in the armpit of an otherwise free-armed head. This is found at Kirklevington and at Middleton (Fig. 161), the latter a large monument but with very late random ring-plait and a shaft not cut into cylinder-shape and yet left blank under a waist-belt of plait. On the edge is a very debased scroll, suggesting perhaps the latest tenth or the eleventh century and a local carver's attempt to vary the common form of which his clients or himself had already begun to tire. That is the excuse, and a sufficient one, for New Art at all periods of history; and it seems to show that there was a good deal of vitality, when circumstances were favourable, even in the decadence of pre-Norman design. The Durham crosses are duffer's work, but the Middleton man was an artist, up to his lights.

Chapter XV. Anglo-Norse

AS Yorkshire was the centre of the Anglo-Danish group of monuments, so was Cumberland of the Anglo-Norse. Among remains of the tenth century and later in this Norse area we can distinguish two classes—those more directly derived from the Anglian survival, and those more characteristically Scandinavian. The first class is represented by the Giant's Thumb at Penrith (Fig. 162) which bears scrolls of so Anglian a character along with a wheel-head, as to suggest (Cumb. and Westmd. Ant. Soc. Trans. N.S. xxiii, 55) the second quarter of the tenth century. One piece of ornament upon it is the braid seen also on the Leeds parish church cross (Fig. 193). This braid is seen also on the Hawsker shaft (Fig. 168) of about that age, Scandinavian by its knot; at Kirklevington and Pickhill, of late tenth or eleventh century; and it seems to be one of the elements used by the master designer of the disc-faced Whithorn group, probably from the middle of the tenth. The Giant's Thumb at any rate is the work of a craftsman bred in Anglian traditions but accepting the wheel-head, perhaps as a novelty.

The second class is more distantly connected with

FIGURE 162

the Anglian survival, for it begins with the Cumbrian version of leaf-scrolls to which it superadds Scandinavian motives. The Cumbrian 'spirals' or stripped and debased scrolls are the work of a small school in a limited area in the west. They occur at Beckermet (Fig. 163), Haile (Fig. 164), St Bees (Fig. 165), Harrington (Fig. 166), Aspatria, Dearham, Isel and Bridekirk (Fig. 118) with a late outlier in east Cumberland at Addingham (Fig. 116-14) and traces of the influence of the school at Whithorn. On some of the crossheads there is the 'lorgnette' which seems to have come in from Yorkshire over Stainmoor. Several of the stones bear also the 'stopped-plait' which connects them with Galloway; it must have been a local invention of the same group of workmen, and not later than the Anglian inscriptions at

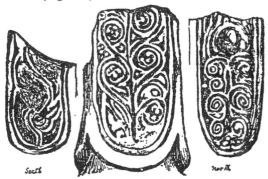

FIGURE 163. ST BRIDGET'S, BECKERMET

Whithorn. The *swastika* on one of these at Aspatria and another at Dearham repeats the symbol we saw on slabs, probably earlier, at Aspatria and Craignarget; and this no doubt was brought by the earliest Norse settlers, already Christianized to some extent, arriving on the Solway somewhere about 920 onwards, though these slabs and the later crosses need not be thought to date to the beginning of the settlement. The churches where they were set up were probably founded by the Norse, who imported such dedications as St Bridget's from Gaelic regions, for there are similar dedications in the two Norse areas of settlement on the two shores of the Solway.

Another token of the same influence is the vertebral or chain-pattern which was used by Gaut Bjarnarson and his school in the Isle of Man from before the middle of the tenth century and thereafter for about a hundred years. The latest Manx example is on the cross-head at Michael, I. o. M. (Kermode's No. 89) which Dr Shetelig classes with the series from about 1000 to about 1040 ('Saga-

FIGURE 164. HAILE

147

book of the Viking Society', ix, 267). It is found also in Sweden, but for our purpose it is enough to point out that it must have reached Cumberland from Man, for its frequency is greatest on the west coast. Like the wheel-heads it travelled over all the Norse area but was unusual among the Anglo-Danes. Examples are found at Muncaster, Gosforth, Crosscanonby, Dearham, Bromfield and Rockcliff (Fig. 159); there is a debased form of it on the so-called Norse cross at St Bees (Fig. 165). By way of

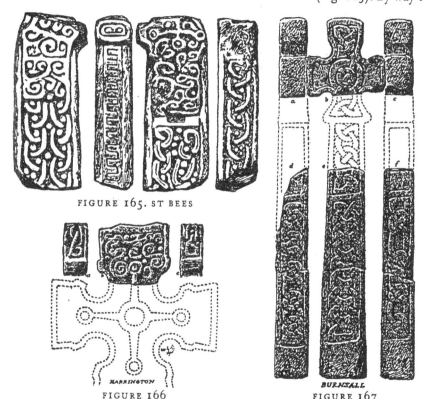

FIGURE 165. ST BEES

FIGURE 166

HARRINGTON

BURNSALL

FIGURE 167

Stainmoor it wandered to Gainford (Fig. 116-20), Croft and Sockburn on the Tees and, overstepping the Cleveland boundary, to Kirkby Moorside, in a patch of country where we have already seen Norse forms invading the edge of Danish territory; but it went no further in that direction. In non-Danish Wharfedale and Airedale it occurs at Burnsall (Fig. 167) and Kildwick, the last perhaps approached by the southern route,

148

along which it is found at Urswick, Lancaster and Melling. There is an outlying example at Warkworth in Northumberland on the back of the very late headstone (Fig. 17e). To the south by a natural route it went to Penmon in Anglesey (Fig. 158) and there is a little bit of it on the Maenychwyfan (Fig. 157) showing the Norse influence in North Wales round about 1000; and southward still, but not outside the Vikings' tracks, at Cardynham in Cornwall on a cross perhaps of late tenth century or eleventh.

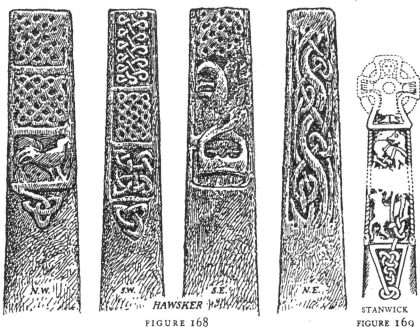

N.W.   S.W.   S.E.   N.E.

HAWSKER

STANWICK

FIGURE 168   FIGURE 169

With this chain-pattern is often found, on the same stone, the Scandinavian ring-knot. As it occurs on the ivory chessmen from the Lewis and on a slab at Holm in the Orkneys it is obviously Norse; and the only place in a Danish area where it is found is Middleton, in that district south of Cleveland where we have already found no hard and fast line between the two races of settlers, and at Middleton (Fig. 161) it is in a very late form. In Cleveland it is seen at Hawsker (Fig. 168) and Kirklevington; in the western area at Melling, Lancaster, Urswick, Aspatria, Bromfield and a late form on the 'warrior's' hogback at Gosforth. On the Maenychwyfan is a fine example, but the Manx did not use it, showing that Cumbrian design was not wholly derived from the Island. This knot is of course to be distinguished from the very common tenth

149

century ring-twist as at Gilling (Fig. 143) from which it might have come *a priori*; it links up the Norse of Northumbria and surrounding parts with some of the northern isles.

The group of the Hart and Hound (or Wolf) is not seen in Yorkshire nearer to the Danish district than Melsonby, where there is a fragment (Fig. 20e) possibly to be so interpreted. Upon the broken cross at Stanwick (Figs. 13-8 and 169) seems to have

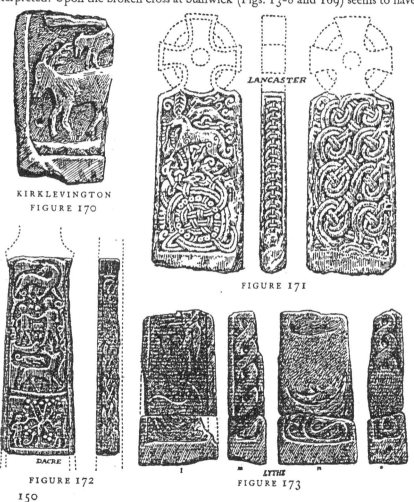

KIRKLEVINGTON
FIGURE 170

LANCASTER

FIGURE 171

FIGURE 172

DACRE

LYTHE
FIGURE 173

been an animal above the hart. Both of these places are on the border beween the Danes of the Vale of Mowbray and the Teesdale Norse. It occurs at Kirklevington in Cleveland (Fig. 170); in lower Wensleydale there is a rude example at Wath. Lancaster can show a very fine stone (Fig. 171) with chain-pattern, Scandinavian knot, dragon-

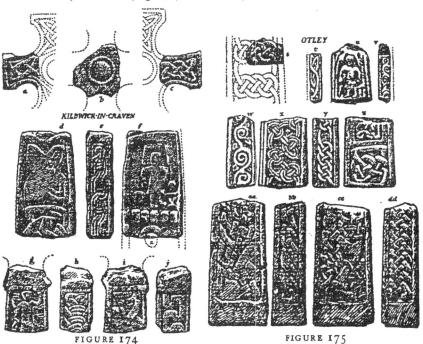

FIGURE 174   FIGURE 175

heads to the plaited straps, and the Hart and Wolf decoratively drawn. At Dacre is a well-known cross-shaft (Fig. 172) with this pair of animals, probably earlier than the last by its general air of Anglian survival, although it shows the tenth century beast with head reverted. At the foot of the shaft we seem to have Adam and Eve with the tree and the serpent, unusually pictorial; higher up are two figures who look as though they were shaking hands, whence it has been supposed that the stone related to the treaty of Dacre or Eamont between Æthelstan and Constantine of Scotland or Owain of Cumbria. For this explanation there are not sufficient reasons; the cross was probably a tenth century grave-monument, and put up to

FIGURE 176

151

a Norse settler, for the Hart and Wolf occur pretty frequently in the Isle of Man. San-dulf's stone at Andreas (Kermode's No. 103) is classed by Dr Shetelig with work about 940; Joalf's slab at Michael (No. 105), the so-called Roolwer cross at Maughold (No. 72) and that at Bride on which Mr Kermode finds the figure of Thor's fishing (No. 97) are of the eleventh century; but all have this animal-group. On the Gosforth cross (Fig. 184) is a variant; the wolf follows the stag, not leaping on its back. On the slab from St Paul's, London (in the Guildhall Museum) is a late decorative rendering of the hart alone. Hunting scenes are frequent on Scottish monuments and a stag alone is occasion-ally seen, but this group is apparently confined to the Scandinavian series we are describing. Its origin may be very remote; something almost exactly like it is figured on a seal from Cyprus (Sagabook of the Viking Soc., ix, 289) though a connexion is not traceable.

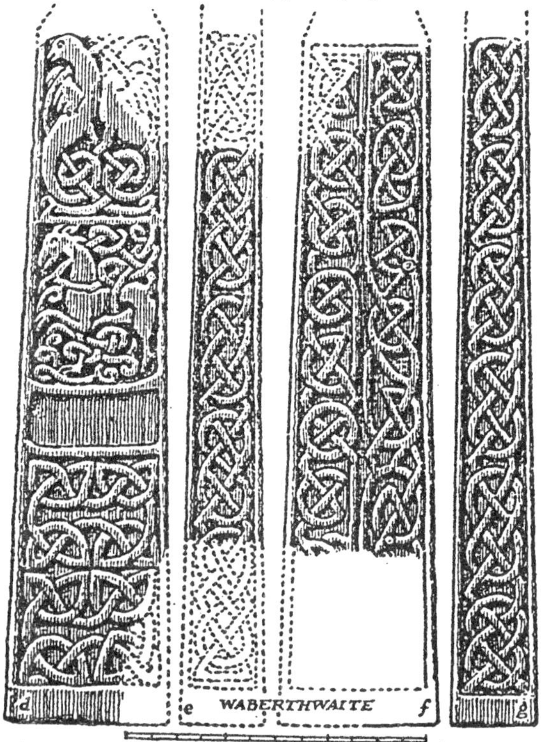

Another motive is the pair of wrestlers seen at Lythe in Cleveland (Fig. 173) recalling wrestlers at Eilean Mòr in the Sound of Jura; Romilly Allen cites other Scottish and Irish examples. The Clephane horn has pairs of wrestlers which Mr O. M. Dalton (*Archae-ologia*, vol. 65, p. 214) classes as Byzantine of the tenth or eleventh century. This would make the idea possible to Vik-ings not unaccustomed to east-ern trade and travel.

The usual style of figure-drawing in the Norse area, late tenth to eleventh century, is seen in the examples from Kild-wick in Craven (Fig. 174), the Otley 'warrior' (Fig. 175) and the quaint angel on a stone formerly at Slaidburn but now lost (Fig. 176), nearly all with humped shoulders and arms a-kimbo. The Manx bird-faces do not appear in Northumbrian carvings, probably because

WABERTHWAITE

FIGURE 177

Scandinavian influence was much less prevailing here than on the Island.

To turn now to some of the more striking examples of the period. The later cross at Waberthwaite in west Cumberland (Fig. 177) keeps touch with its Anglian origin, or more particularly with models in south-west Yorkshire, probably through Lancaster, by its use of the Carrick bend and the four Stafford knots linked on a ring; but its treatment of the materials, with rings in the plait and considerable irregularity, is tenth century. The quasi-Jellinge birds and horse are not very far gone in conventional development. This must have been made about or soon after the middle of the century, when the old church or cell at the place was not destroyed by the new settlers but retained by them, as they seem to have done also at Urswick, where they set up a wheel-head cross of which a fragment, enough to show its general character, was found in 1913. At Glassonby, Hutton-in-the-Forest and Gilcrux other fragments of this kind were found, transitional from late Anglian to the Viking Age style.

At Aspatria, now in the church but formerly standing in its own base in the churchyard, is a shaft (Fig. 178) with part of the wheel-head, a little nearer to the more developed Scandinavian style. It has the ring-knot, a quasi-Jellinge beast at the foot, and random plait on one side; but on the other and on the edge the plaits are regular, almost Angglian. The head (see p. 143f) makes it late tenth century.

Another example of this transition can be restored from a fragment at Melling in Lonsdale (Fig. 179) with a fine ring-knot and traces of chain-pattern on the edge. It might be by the same hand as the Lancaster Hart and Hound stone (Fig. 171) which has similar features, *plus* the animals; and on this last there seems to be

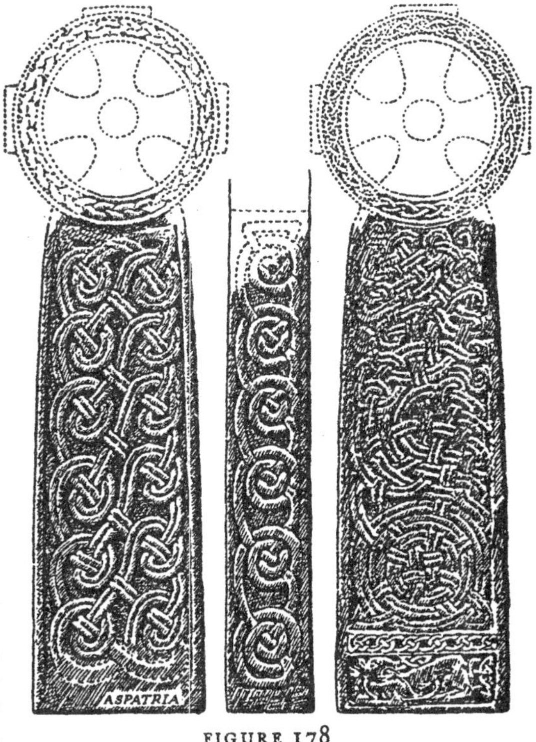

FIGURE 178

153

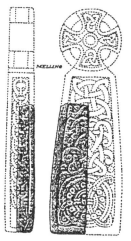

FIGURE 179

HEXHAM
found 1870
(niche 10.)

FIGURE 181

154

HEXHAM: Cross found 1908.

FIGURE 180

a small fragment of the spring of a wheel-head. But the plait is simply an Anglian form developed with snake-heads at the ends of the straps.

This is seen rather strikingly in the two late crosses at Hexham. The one found in 1908 (Fig. 180) has no trace of a wheel to the head; its patterns are simply Anglian, but late Anglian; it has even an arch which usually means a saint underneath. On the back there are the feet of a bird, probably a standing eagle and therefore one of the four symbols of the evangelists. But the treatment shows that this cross cannot have been made before the burning of the church in 875. It was put up over a burial at the ruined site, and perhaps not before 900, because Hexham was a district in which Anglian tradition died hard. On the other hand, the cross found there in 1870 (Fig. 181) has just the same character except that the plaits end in snake-heads and in one case in a nearly complete little beast. At the neck of the cross is an animal, to be seen plainly in the raking light of a fine evening: it has lost its head but appears to be meant for a lion of sorts — one of the evangelist symbols again. This cross must be well advanced in the tenth century; it was put up while the church was still a ruin, and Hexham still clung to its Anglian character, not being so near the Norse settlements which gave a Scandinavian character to Lancaster and Melling.

Returning to West Cumberland we must look at the cross, with a head which may or may not be its own, now affixed to the same base, at Muncaster near Waberthwaite (Fig. 182). The shaft is altogether occupied by one great chain-pattern. On the back is a big plait of four strands, tending to angularity and therefore late in the tenth century. We are beginning to lose touch with Anglian origins, and here we may be under

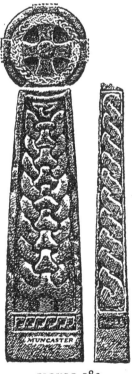

FIGURE 182

FIGURE 183. BRIGHAM

Manx influence, because Muncaster is close to the great harbour, only forty miles of sailing from the Island.

At Brigham near Cockermouth is a remarkable cross-base (Fig. 183) deeply and smoothly carved with dragon-esque plaits, quasi-Jellinge but apparently rather late and with no tokens of Anglian influence in the design.

The cross at Gosforth (Cumberland) ranks, on the Anglian side, with the round-shaft series of which we have shown examples in Chapter II (Fig. 12-2). It was carved by a late-Anglian craftsman, for no other in those parts could adopt and carry out this peculiar and difficult form of monument. Its wheel-head is based on the Northumbrian, non-Celtic shape, and in being a wheel-head it differs from the Penrith Giant's Grave crosses, though otherwise closely connected by its 'staff-rood' character. It is connected with Penrith also by the cable-frame to the crucifix, which occurs round the angel of the Giant's Thumb. But at Gosforth the Norse element in the population asked for design to suit the local taste. The chain-pattern is almost overloaded on the stone; it occurs in three different forms, including the pleached variety which embraces the upper part of the round shaft, and is seen again at Dearham and Cross-canonby. The design (Fig. 184) suggests models in wood-carving, followed by the mason, who after shaping his stone in an accustomed way has given himself up to carrying out his orders; and in doing so has lost count of the fact that his cross was

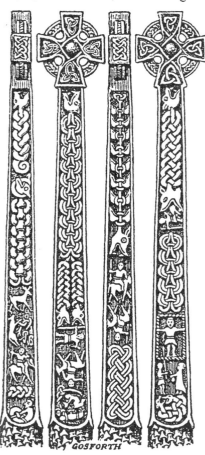

GOSFORTH

FIGURE 184

going to be up-ended—just as the carver of the Sheffield archer did. Some of the figures obviously meant to stand upright seem to be lying suspended in the air, and in the case of the pair of horsemen fighting and in that of a horseman attacking the figure with the horn (Vidar?) the designer has given in to the exigences of a space too narrow for the display of a group. This means that a 'literary subject' was set for him to illustrate. What that subject was may still be doubtful, but it has been suggested ('Cumbd. and Westmd. Ant. Soc. Transactions', N.S. xvii, 99ff) that if we begin on the south side at the foot of the shaft, go round with the sun and up and down the sides alternately, we get a remarkable parallel to the chief events told in the Völuspá in the Edda:—(1) Chaos, creation by Odin, and Eikthyrnir (the Hart); (2) the wars of the gods and giants and the three pledges, Heimdal, Odin and Baldr, the last shown by Loki's punishment for taking Baldr's life; (3) Ragnarök and the attack on the gods; (4) the new world with Vidar slaying the Fenris-wolf and the promise of the rebirth of Baldr, here identified with Christ. This explanation at any rate might tally with the folk-theology of about 1000, when the Völuspá was current, especially at such a centre of Norse life as Gosforth must then have been; and if it is illusory, we still have before us in this monument something that needs explanation in the light of all we know about the time and place. But as to type, the cross is not Manx, nor Scottish, Irish or Welsh; it is a development of general Northumbrian art under strong Norse influences, and its period must be about the turn of the tenth into the eleventh century.

Dearham cross (Fig. 185) confirms this dating, for it has one of the 'eared' heads which we have seen to be of that time, and it repeats the pleached chain pattern in an unmistakable way. Whether this form of the pattern has any significance, such as a conventional rendering of the tree of Yggdrasil (as the late Rev W. S. Calverley thought) is not to our present purpose;

DEARHAM

FIGURE 185

FIGURE 186. GREAT CLIFTON

the use of the same form to cover the roof of the Crosscanonby hogback may be thought to militate against this theory, though in the case of Dearham cross the whole pattern springs, as Mr Calverley observed, from a kind of tree-stem.

The last of this group we need mention is the remarkable shaft at Great Clifton near Workington where the back and edge are covered with fairly regular but bifurcated plaitwork. The front, however, bears a very wild design of late Scandinavian

157

character (Fig. 186). In the middle of the shaft is a little human being riding on a snake; similar motives are seen at Gosforth and Penrith (Figs. 198, 212), conceivably explicable as a symbol of Hell and Christ's descent thereto. Beside this figure is a plaited snake with a human head; doubtful as indicating the story of Gunnar in the worm-close, for there is no *fidla* which Gunnar ought to be playing upon. And beneath another huge serpent is a hooded or nimbed figure tied up in plaited snakes; if nimbed, possibly Christ himself in Hades. But then, what becomes of the famous Kirkby

KIRKBY STEPHEN

FIGURE 187

Stephen 'bound devil' (Fig. 187)? This indeed has been called a devil only because the ornamental volutes (snakes?) near his head look like horns, and the interpreters of dreams have translated him into Loki. One thing we can say of this last —the gable form beneath him is that which we see in such late crosses as at Whalley (Fig. 132); it is part of the lost subject on the lower reach of the shaft. It therefore connects our Scandinavian types once more with their source in the late Anglian, which survived the time when the Kirkby Stephen figure was carved—about late tenth century—along the line of the Stainmoor road.

We must now turn to another series, starting in western Yorkshire. At Collingham (Fig. 188) and Kirkby Wharfe (Fig. 189) are late shafts with a trellis like that figured by Cattaneo from Cimitile near Nola and attributed by him to the beginning of the eighth century ('Architecture in Italy, fifth to eleventh centuries', Fig. 27). It faintly resembles the Hexham double scroll, and in badly drawn instances, such as at Guiseley and Barwick-in-Elmet, might be supposed to have been so derived. But it differs in the fact that the tendrils of the pattern do not spring from it but cross it, being therefore a trellis and not a vine-branch. Now at Staveley in the West Riding is a late fan-armed cross (Fig. 190) with this pattern and also the bouquet ornament known as Ringerike style, which, whatever its provenance, means in Scandinavia the early part of the

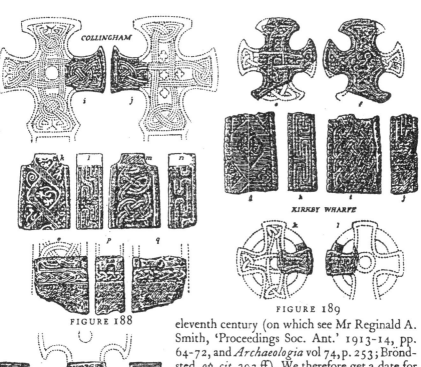

FIGURE 189

FIGURE 188

STAVELEY
FIGURE 190

eleven century (on which see Mr Reginald A. Smith, 'Proceedings Soc. Ant.' 1913-14, pp. 64-72, and *Archaeologia* vol 74, p. 253; Brøndsted, *op. cit.* 293 ff). We therefore get a date for the Staveley cross and its curious group of figures, very dimly seen on the stone with the help of a raking light.

Allied to this is the 'Sigurd' shaft at Halton near Lancaster (Fig. 191). Here we have the trellis, along with a definite imitation of previous crosses (Fig. 92) at the same place, in its arches and angel; and reminiscences of Nunburnholme in the figures under the angel, and of Waberthwaite (which connected with Lancaster) in the horse, and perhaps in the pair of dragons, replacing the Waberthwaite birds, on another side. It may be remarked that the 'bite' out of the arris, seen chiefly on this side, is certainly original;

159

the designer has made the most of his defective material, not being able to get a better stone. On the fourth side is the story of Sigurd the Völsung unmistakably portrayed, as on various Manx crosses:—the smith at his forge, and again with his head off; above, Sigurd sucking his thumb while he roasts the dragon's heart; and at the top the birds telling him the story of the treasure. On this

FIGURE 191

FIGURE 192. ST JOHN'S, BECKERMET

LEEDS
CHURCH

W   FIGURE 193   161

side the figures resemble those of the Gosforth cross; like it, the Halton cross has a story to tell; and though this monument has been dated later, it seems to fall by its connexions into the same busy period, not much past the year 1000.

At Burnsall in Wharfedale is a fan-armed cross (Fig. 108) with a piece of shaft almost certainly belonging to it and bearing the Ringerike motive, perhaps in an early form. At St John's, Beckermet in west Cumberland there are two such pieces with a base perhaps belonging to one cross (Fig. 192) considerably more advanced in style and very rich in their ornamentation, showing the Norse art of the eleventh century in a district that now seems out-of-the-way but in those times was the centre of the wide-spreading region controlled by the sea-faring Northmen.

LEEDS MUSEUM

FIGURE 194

Leeds, we have noticed (p. 52), was about 940-950 the *confinium Normannorum atque Cumbrorum*, border-town between the Danish settlements and the region over which Cumbrian kings and their friends claimed sway. At the parish church (Fig. 193) recovered by the late Major R. W. Moore, and Dr John Rawlinson Ford, happily still with us, is a great cross (more fully described in the Thoresby Society's *Miscellanea*, vol. xxii, pp. 267 ff) which, Dr Bröndsted has remarked, bears the Ringerike pattern and must be after 1000. If so, it is curious to observe the persistence of the Anglian scroll with leaves and berry bunches, though much stiffened, and Anglian plaits not very much debased. The Ringerike pattern (at the top of the third side) is also curious because it has all the appearance of being a development of the Scandinavian ring-knot and the question arises,—how far was this development effected on British soil?

The figures on this Leeds cross more nearly resemble those of Celtic MSS. than any we have seen. Considering the connexion between Yorkshire and Ireland, closer than

162

ver in the tenth century, some borrowing may be understood. The man with a sword
nd a bird (hawk?) on his shoulder we take as a portrait, like the man with two birds
t Kirklevington, the seated warrior at Nunburnholme and other armed men at Otley
nd Brailsford; it was the effigy of the person to whom the cross was erected and it has
o mythological attribute. On the other hand the group at the foot of the first side can
ardly be anything but Völund the smith seizing Bödvild; his artificial wings and smithy
ools are plain to see; and this is corroborated by the cross which can be restored (Fig.
94) from fragments at Leeds Museum, obviously a duplicate of the parish church

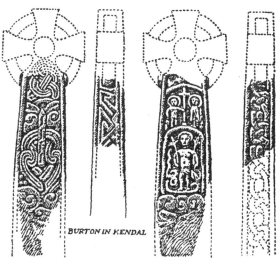

BURTON IN KENDAL

FIGURE 195

cross in this respect, and
upplying some of the de-
ails of the lower part. The
igures of a person with a
ook at the top, and a saint
John the Evangelist?) in
he middle, are as far gone
n debased stylizing as such
work can go; but the gen-
ral effect of the monu-
ment, with its regular
Anglian plait-work, must
warn us against putting it
very late.

One more cross we must
notice as of this group is
hat (Fig. 195) at the
church of Burton, between
Lancaster and Kendal. It
differs from all the rest in
ts key-pattern, suggesting some influence from the north where key-pattern was in
favour, although it had been sparingly in use from the ninth century in Northumbria.
On the front we have Christ in Resurrection or in the Descent into Hell, symbolized
by the serpent trodden under foot—a hint, perhaps, on former puzzles. Above are SS.
Mary and John by the empty cross, as at Kirkby Wharfe. We do not know that a church
existed at Burton until the time of William Rufus, but this cross must put back the
clock a little and give us reason to date the foundation as definitely pre-Norman.

And, connected by its key-pattern, we have at Winwick in Lancaster the elaborate
cross-head already noticed (Fig. 155) as a work of the Anglo-Norse style with very
strong colouring from the Celto-Norse district; though even so not entirely foreign. It
cannot be considered as quite unconnected with the series we have traced from early
efforts, still holding the hand of the Anglian survival, to these late displays of decorative innovation.

Chapter XVI. Hogbacks

ALTHOUGH they are not crosses, the hogbacks of Northumbria are so closely related to standing monuments that they must not be passed over. By a hogback is meant a recumbent tombstone in the shape of a low, long house of which the roof-tree is slightly arched lengthwise. There were many shrine-tombs of ordinary forms earlier and later. Bede describes the sepulchre of St Chad as a wooden monument made like a little house with a roof and a hole in the wall through which people used to put a hand and take some of the dust, valued as medicine. So, as in the case of all stone crosses, a wooden version came first; and it is fairly obvious that the stone hogback was an imitation of the model of a cottage built on siles or A-shaped timbers roughly thus—aA : Aa —the biggest pair of siles in the middle, and where the colon is the door would be. A low wall was made up with clay daubing to enclose the legs of the A, and the steep roof was thatched or shingled. Such buildings were common in the north, if not elsewhere, until the eighteenth century.

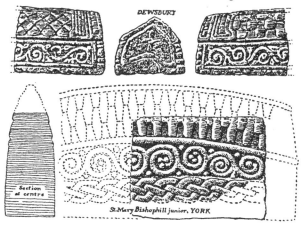

DEWSBURY

Section at centre

St Mary Bishophill junior, YORK

FIGURE 196

The hogback tombstone was well known before the Danish invasion. At Dewsbury Church and York Museum (Hospitium No. 8) there are parts of such (Fig. 196) with good Anglian ornament of the third quarter of the ninth century. A fragment, apparently similar, is in Leeds Museum. There were two at Crathorne (Fig. 197) on the edge of Cleveland (one now at

CRATHORNE

FIGURE 197

Durham) with scrolls which might be of the end of the ninth century. At Bedale is part of a hogback with late but symmetrical plaits and on one gable-end a rude carving of what looks like the Madonna and Child; a similar fragment is at Oswaldkirk with the Virgin standing and holding the Babe in her arms. Among these we do not include mere coped graveslabs, nor the very irregular forms found in Scotland, Wales and Cornwall, which are sometimes catalogued as hogbacks; but we may mention a small example from Ingleby Arncliffe at the York Museum (Hospitium No. 15). The roof of this seems never to have been ornamented; the sides have been scabbled and any patterns lost; but just as very small graveslabs were sometimes made in post-Conquest times, rather because the means or materials failed for making them full-size, so this hogback may not have been intended to set over a child's grave. Or perhaps it may: but another diminutive hogback from Falstone (Blackgate Museum, Newcastle) has the statement inscribed both in minuscules and in Anglian runes that 'Eomert set [this] after Hroethbert, a monument to his uncle; pray for his soul.' It looks as though a man called Uncle Robert must have grown up before he died; in which case the size of the stone had nothing to do with the size of the grave. At any rate the length of a hogback is not anthropological evidence.

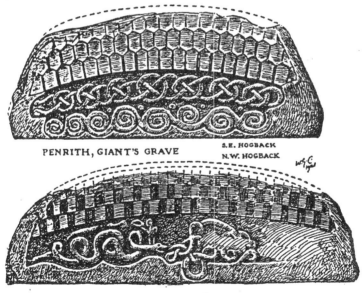

PENRITH, GIANT'S GRAVE   S.E. HOGBACK
                             N.W. HOGBACK

FIGURE 198

We shall come soon to a number of hogbacks with bears on their gable ends, but first it may be convenient to mention some which have no such appendages. These perhaps represent the ordinary, older type, though they are by no means always early in date. One of those at the Penrith Giant's Grave (Figs. 198, 199), with an Anglian scroll, had certainly no gable-ornament: one at Lowther, with a Viking army and

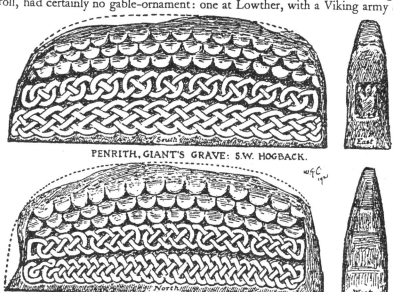

PENRITH, GIANT'S GRAVE: S.W. HOGBACK.

FIGURE 199

ship carved on its wall (Fig. 210), had none; the Abercorn stone, a true hogback though it has no walls but is all tegulated roof, had none; so also one of those at Sockburn-on-Tees, and the very rude stone at Helmsley church (Fig. 54*b*). A still ruder hogback is in Harrogate Museum from Pippin Castle (Fig. 200) with runes of about 1100.* Many are mutilated at the ends and may be left out of count, as at Kirkby

FIGURE 200

* Probably reading—] SUNA S[in, *i.e.* '. . . his son' ('Yorks. Archaeol. Journ.' xxiii, 182).

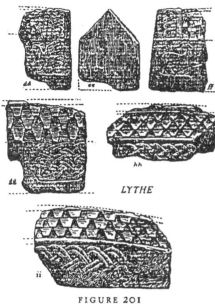

LYTHE

FIGURE 201

Stephen and Bolton-le-Sands. Appleby St Michael's, Bromfield and Crosscanonby churches have hogbacks built into the masonry as lintels and consequently obscured. The late hogbacks at Gosforth, Aspatria, Hexham and West Kirby in Cheshire had no bears. At Stonegrave in Ryedale and at Lythe in Cleveland are groups of hogbacks (Figs. 201, 202 and 203) with tenth to eleventh century plaits and figures, but among these only one example, at Lythe, and that a very late one, has anything on the gable. This has the top of the ridge at the end hacked into an ugly face. Another, at Barmston in the East Riding, has a still uglier face (Fig. 204) a little more in relief. And at Easington in Cleveland that position is occupied by a large snake's head, rather realistic.

What the snake's head meant, more than ornament, we do not know. At a guess it might be said that it was intended to scare away evil spirits; but in all true Northumbrian hogbacks the heads look inwards; and if they were warders of the tomb one would expect them to turn the other way and face the enemy. But it was very much in the taste of the tenth century to put a head at the end of anything as a finial; even a pre-Danish graveslab at Knells from Carlisle has a little animal on one upper corner; the other corner is broken. Perhaps one need look no further for the queer fancy that made the muzzled bear climb on the roofs of these houses of the dead.

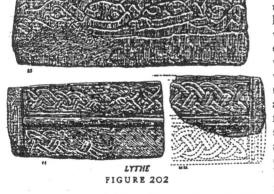

LYTHE

FIGURE 202

167

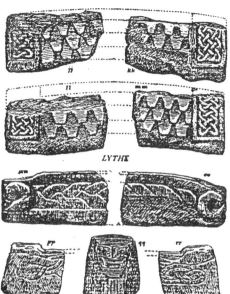

BARMSTON

FIGURE 204

BROMPTON

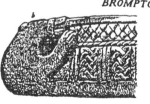

FIGURE 205

LYTHE

FIGURE 203

Brompton, near Northallerton, is the great centre of the bear type (Fig. 205). Here no less than ten different examples existed, five of which are now at Durham (Cathedral Library, lviii-lxii) with another which is mutilated and perhaps had no bear. They are different from each other in the sense of being separately designed, not repeating the same model. In most of these the tegulated roof, usual in hogbacks, is absent, replaced by other ornament; but the patterns used, except in Durham lxii, which seems later, are of the second half of the tenth century. The bears are almost as natural as Bernese wood-carvings; the tamed and muzzled beast was evidently a familiar sight. Only in one case (Durham lviii) is there the conventional joint-spiral in a work of the Brompton school; and when we think of the stylized Anglian and still more sty-

168

lized Jellinge animals, this sudden outburst of straightforward representation is most surprising. It would be bewildering if we did not know that artistic genius is a very curious and unaccountable phenomenon, springing up where it is least expected and interfering with the course of art-history when that course has been too pedantically laid down. There cannot be any doubt that, in the middle of the hide-bound conventionalists of the later tenth century, an artist appeared with an idea all his own—or he thought so, not knowing how many others had been and would be in like case. And one can hardly help hearing him say—'My trick? Oh, it is very simple. What I always tell my lads is "Go straight to nature. That is all."' But artists never can explain. They do their work and others try to imitate them, but not by going to nature.

There was plenty of imitation, following this new discovery. One example from Arncliffe (Durham No. lxiv) must have been made by the Brompton carvers. At Stainton-in-Cleveland there is a good bear; at Sinnington another. At Osmotherley is a hogback with a rather poor bear, and on the ridge a step-pattern, later than the T⊥T on some of the Brompton stones. Wycliffe-on-Tees has parts of two, both falling back into conventional treatment. The lost hogback at Kirkby Malzeard, destroy-

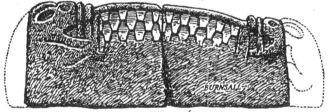

FIGURE 206

ed by a fire in 1908, seems to have been nearer the original type but not a Brompton work. Burnsall had three, two of which are very mutilated, but the third (Fig. 206) shows the bears, passably imitated, with their muzzles emphasised. Pickhill has two; one with a bear more like a rat, and the other with only the two feet of its bear (one on each side) remaining, but on the hogback-wall a quasi-Jellinge creature, with

FIGURE 207. HEYSHAM

double outline and joint-spiral complete, showing the incomplete fusion of two styles (Fig. 141). At Sockburn-on-Tees is one of the Brompton type, and (beside that formerly mentioned) another somewhat like the famous example at Heysham near Lancaster.

The Heysham hogback (Fig. 207) has attracted attention by its 'literary subject', which has been variously explained. If we could accept the interpretation given by the late Dr H. Colley March we should see in it an illustration of the Völuspá, as at Gosforth: on one side the Norse gods in their last fight at Ragnarök and on the other the 'One who should come' to restore order in the new world. And then we should date it to about 1000, when these tidings were in the air, and a general impression was felt that the end of the world was at hand with the millenium of peace to follow (see *e.g.* Freeman, 'Norman Conquest', i, 307). With this date the style—or want of it— does not contend. The bears are very debased bears and the whole work is rude.

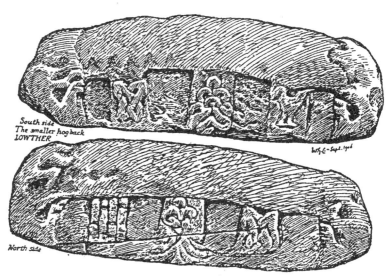

South side
The smaller hogback
LOWTHER

North side

FIGURE 208

At Lowther churchyard in Westmorland there is one more bear-hogback (Fig. 208) of about the beginning of the eleventh century, to judge from the quasi-Ringerike bouquet on one side; and as there is often an outlier to a group we find our last example so far away as Inchcolm in the Firth of Forth, with a tegulated roof and a figure with hands up, repeating the Heysham motive.

It remains only to notice a few late hogbacks, bearless but interesting. In the Museum at West Kirby at the mouth of the Dee is a rudely cut stone with late open plait on the side walls, and on the roof tegulae which have lost the regular form of tiles, and look more like gum-drops exuding from a fir-tree. A curious pattern which follows the ridge of the stone, pairs of rings with a bar thrust through them, is rather like

170

the buckle-knot on eleventh century cross-heads at Kirkdale (N. Riding). There is a kind of local tradition or belief that this monument was brought from Ireland; but according to Romilly Allen there are no hogbacks in Ireland. The source of the stone used is unknown. It was probably carved on the spot by someone who had seen hogbacks of the bearless type and was trying to recover his memories of them.

FIGURE 209

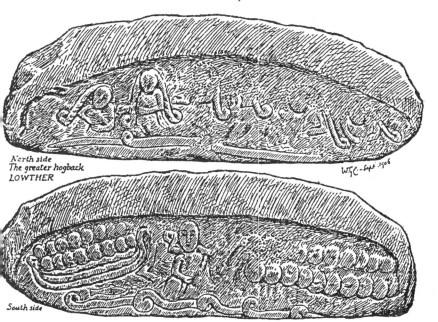

North side
The greater hogback
LOWTHER

South side

FIGURE 210

At Aspatria, now in the church, is part of a very elaborately ornamented monument (Fig. 209) cleverly carved though the plaits are roughly picked. Above the two rows of neatly cut tegulae, each bearing a *triquetra*, is a sharp, steep ridge with angular

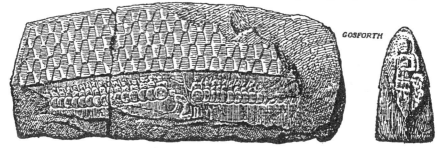

FIGURE 211

twist on its sides, and on the eaves a step-pattern; the walls are divided into bays by pilasters, richly covered with plaits. By these it appears to be of the earlier half of the eleventh century, and Norse by the ring-knot.

Beside the bear hogback at Lowther there are two more; one with a row of female figures on each side, with snakes beneath, possibly (as Calverley suggested) the Descent into Hades. The other (Fig. 210) has similar figures and snake on one side, and on

FIGURE 212

the reverse a figure standing between an army with shields on his left and a Viking ship on his right. For fear of any mistake the carver has put the fish in the sea, and the snake below must be the sea-serpent.

172

At Gosforth (Cumbd.) in 1896 a hogback was discovered in the foundations of the church; another was got out in the year following. The first (Fig. 211) because it bears an interesting sculpture of two armies meeting, and on the wall of the gable-end the figure of a warrior, has been called the 'Warrior's Tomb'. One side is covered with a random plait based on large rings and at the sinister end of this panel is a figure like that on the Leeds cross in which a Scandinavian ring-knot seems to be caught in the act of blossoming into a Ringerike bouquet. This perhaps warns us against dating the stone much later than 1000. The other (Fig. 212) which has been called the 'Saint's Tomb' because it bears a crucifix on the end, has the roof key-patterned but not tegulated, and bordered with a frame of plait. On the walls are great serpents and small human figures wrestling with them—a motive seen also on a Penrith hogback (Fig. 198) but here carved with great skill in high relief. It should be remarked that although this stone is generally like the series of hogbacks, its ridge (which is much broken) does not curve more than very slightly, if at all. This is definitely later work than the 'Warrior's Tomb'; Dr Bröndsted, finding an analogy in treatment of similar motives at Eskilstuna in Sweden, of about 1050, suggests a date after the middle of the

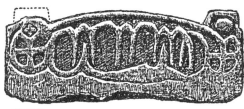

century (*op. cit.* 227f). That is a period for which West Cumberland history fails us: whether any connexion with Sweden is possible we are unable to say; but the work on the 'Saint's Tomb' was carried out by a very efficient sculptor.

The last of the hogbacks is the clumsy thing at Hexham church (Fig. 213), hardly a work of art but most interesting from the historical evidence it supplies. On one side is an attempt at intersecting arches, which are seen first in a capital at Lastingham of about 1078 (information from Mr John Bilson; 'Archaeologia Aeliana', fourth series, i, 92), and were introduced architecturally at Durham Cathedral in 1093. This gives

FIGURE 213

a reason for dating the stone to the last quarter of the eleventh century, and the period when Eilaf was restoring the church at Hexham. It brings us up to the Anglo-Norman overlap, on which something remains to be said before we have finished our review of the pre-Norman age.

173

Chapter XVII. Outcomes of Northumbrian Monumental Art

NOT long ago there was still much doubt as to the dating of late pre-Norman. It was uncertain how long the making of such crosses lasted in Northumbria and how the interlaced patterns fared at the close of the period. We knew that plaits, in modified forms, were used in the twelfth century and later, but it was generally supposed that Norman influence rapidly effaced the old style, and that anything of the kind ought to be dated before 1100, if not before the Conquest.

Much light, however, has been thrown upon the subject lately by Mr John Bilson, whose papers on Weaverthorpe Church (*Archaeologia*, vol. 72) and on Wharram-le-Street and St Rule's (*Ibid*. vol. 73) showed that old-fashioned work was executed by old-fashioned Northumbrian masons during the second decade of the twelfth century, not only in Yorkshire but as far away as at St Andrews in Scotland. Recently also an examination of Monkwearmouth Church has revealed the comparative lateness of the fabric. It is not the nearly untouched Anglian of Benedict Biscop, and the figures and animals there carved must be coeval with the eleventh century restoration at Hexham. They are of the Anglo-Norman overlap; that is to say, old traditions carried on under

South

East
RASTRICK
FIGURE 214

North

new conditions when the Conquest was politically, but not yet socially, an accomplished fact. A number of stones found at Lindisfarne, with animal-forms that could not antedate the introduction of Jellinge style, and much key-pattern and florid ornament, come under this heading; they are of a dark period about which we have little evidence except that of the monuments themselves, but that evidence is conclusive against placing them earlier than the Danish invasion, at any rate. With other remains in the northern part of Northumbria they illustrate the connexion between Anglian art and the art of the Scottish crosses.

As illustrating the age of decadence two or three examples may be taken from South Yorkshire. In the Rastrick base (Fig. 214), which in a sense may have been imitated from the earlier cross-base at Walton, not far away (Fig. 65), there is a debased treescroll with trefoil leaves, never seen earlier in our examples but matching a design at Birstall (Fig. 224), and poor, loose plait is used to fill one side. On the font

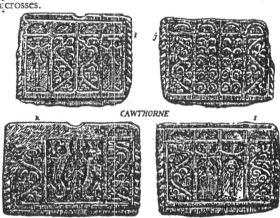

CAWTHORNE

FIGURE 215

now at Cawthorne Church are the same trefoil leaves (Fig. 215) and the tree-scroll we see again at Kirkby Grindalythe (Fig. 217). There is a new shape of cross on the old Anglian model, with rectangular armpits, together with very debased Jellinge beasts,

MIRFIELD

FIGURE 216

meaning long-continued local survival of motives then ancient; for both the history of the place and the form of the font suggest that this was made within the earlier part of the twelfth century. So also the curious headstone at Mirfield (Fig. 216) with its gridiron and reminiscence of motives already seen in examples of Anglian survival. These show the better kind of work that could be done in the Anglo-Norman overlap, technically not despicable but artistically far gone in decay.

As a more convincing instance, because the church and its remains are dated with

175

Mr John Bilson's help, take Kirkby Grindalythe, recent in 1131. Here we have a cross-head and two shaft-fragments (Fig. 217) which show valuable details of the overlap. In neat and skilful workmanship there is a head of 'Celtic' form with a debased tree-scroll and much unornamented ground only incised with the Anglian moulding-lines, easily distinguishable from true mouldings of any architectural style. There is a bifurcated plait which does not preserve sequence, and basket-plait with strong angularity. These, now that we can date

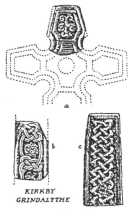

KIRKBY
GRINDALYTHE

FIGURE 217.

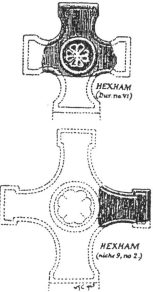

HEXHAM
(Dur. na VI)

HEXHAM
(niche 9, no 2.)

FIGURE 218

them, give us the key to a considerable series and lead to some interesting results.

Of cross-heads entirely plain except for the Anglian mouldings and sometimes a rosette in the centre we have two at Hexham (Fig. 218) and another (Fig. 219) showing a tendency to evade the rich surface-filling of older days, which was then in decadence, as the bit of shaft drawn below it (Fig. 219) bears witness. The last head may be of mid-eleventh century and the plain heads of the close. Other plain heads are at Dewsbury (Fig. 106), Ilkley, Easington,

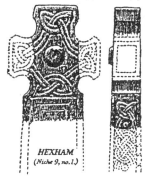

HEXHAM
(Niche 9, no.1.)

HEXHAM
(Dur. Cath. Lib. no. VII.)

176   FIGURE 219

Gilling, Finghall, High Hoyland (Fig. 99), Kildale, Kirkburton (Fig. 125 with the crucifix). Edges of shafts merely moulded are not uncommon and indicate the setting in of the tendency during the eleventh century. Such stones are usually well carved; they are not rude work; they mean the survival of older ornamental forms and they help towards the history of sites in a dark period.

In ruder work the same evasion of trouble is seen in another way. The 'Eoh' stone at Kirkheaton (Fig. 67) has on its edge an angular twist, fairly well done. The Anglian runes do not allow us to place it very late, and the fact that the edge was carved out into relief suggests that the monument was regarded as finished. But part of the field is occupied with sketchy incised volutes. Earlier in date some parts of crosses were left merely sketched, as at Ilkley museum on an Anglian shaft (Fig. 49); and perhaps at about the same time as Eoh certain carvers of the Whithorn school forgot, or were too hurried by their employers, to finish panels they had laid out (Figs. 84, 85). The Nigg

FIGURE 220

stone shows the same incompletion. But this of Eoh is not in that class, and others bear out this judgment. At Kippax near Leeds, on one face of a shaft (Fig. 220), that is obviously meant to be finished, are the same incised volutes; so also with the Middlesmoor cross and the Mexborough shaft (Fig. 112), and a fragment at Sprotborough (both places in the Don valley). And that it was not a trick local to south Yorkshire is shown by the Cheadle cross from Cheshire (York Museum, Hospitium No. 17) where three sides of the shaft are 'ornamented' in this way, and the rest is fairly well carved

in relief (Fig. 221). From the fan-shaped arms this Cheadle cross must be either very late tenth or more likely eleventh century work.

Sketchy ornament like this leads the way to a still more debased kind, which might be fancied early and tentative if we did not collect and compare examples. The shaft (Fig. 222) at Ecclesfield (south Yorks.) does not seem to be merely prepared for carving and then

y

FIGURE 221   177

abandoned, though it is partly covered with incised lines. Among them are wheel-crosses slightly relieved by sinking the spandrels. Now these resemble the same features

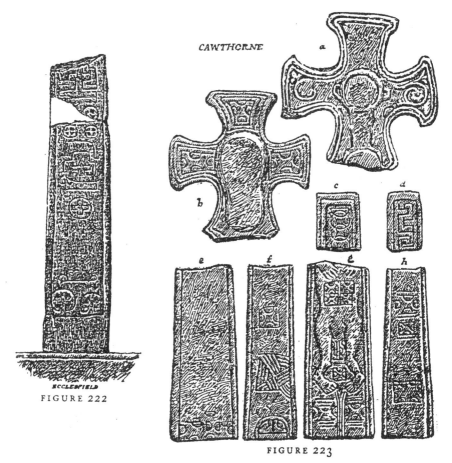

CAWTHORNE

FIGURE 222

FIGURE 223

on the Hexham hogback (Fig. 213), which gives the end of the eleventh century as possible date for Ecclesfield.

On the top of the Hexham hogback is a device made of a kind of D-pattern. We find it again on the great cross at Cawthorne (Fig. 223) at an early Norman site, and

178

nce more on the shaft-fragment (Fig. 112) at Penistone (near Sheffield), dating them and showing that the motive was not confined to one particular neighbourhood.

A step further in labour-saving and we get rustication. Anyone who has tried in a hurry to draw an interlaced pattern knows how difficult it is to get a summary and impressionistic rendering of a subject that must be either thought out or left alone. But to fill the ground with a criss-cross scribble, pretending to give the effect of plait-work, is possible; and this is what some of the later carvers seem to have done. At Kirby Hill is the fragment of a cross-shaft with irregular volutes trailing off into a rude complication like the crackling on an old glazed pot. One feels that the carver had never faced the trouble of drawing a proper plait; it is like a child's letter before he has learnt to write, showing that this cross is obviously a debased copy of the earlier work at the site. At Wath near Ripon the ground of two clumsy figures is filled out in this way. At Adel near Leeds where there is nothing else earlier than the Norman church, is a headstone (Fig. 17k) with rustication only but quite carefully done; the carver has rounded off each incised line to make the little compartments slightly *bombés*, each with its own little pit neatly sunk in the middle. It is not archaic; still less archaistic, for no primitive style is imitated. It is intended to be quite a nice piece of work in a definite style, originating in shorthand for plait.

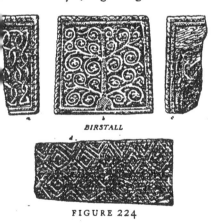

BIRSTALL

FIGURE 224

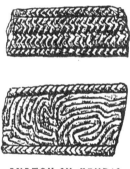

BURTON-IN-KENDAL
FIGURE 225

The shorthand for key-pattern can be also produced. It occurs in the slab at Birstall (Fig. 224d), similarly treated with care and finish. And at Burton-in-Kendal there is part of a cross-shaft with one side elaborately rusticated and the other as carefully zig-zagged, and a neat double cable along the arris (Fig. 225). This double cable is like that on the hammerhead cross at Addingham (Fig. 116-14) the latest of the Cum-

179

brian 'spiral' crosses, and of the same class with the Kilmorie stone from the Rhynns of Galloway (Fig. 113), in which we have seen the last flickers of Anglian survival in transformation to the Scottish cross-slab.

These give us a hint for dating a group in Galloway which otherwise might be put

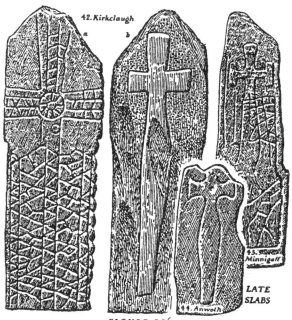

FIGURE 226

down as 'Celtic' and primitive. On the Kirkclaugh and Minnigaff stones (Fig. 226) there is the same rustication; and when we know that both stones belong to Norman mottes, for both must have come from the chapels (at Minnigaff surviving, at Kirkclaugh lost except for the name) of Norman settlers, the mist clears and we see them take their place at about 1100. Further, on the back of the Kirkclaugh stone is a cross with a swollen shaft; so also is the slab at Anwoth, which though unornamented must belong to the same class, and the Hilbre slab at the West Kirby museum.

Mention has already been made of the Corbridge and York finials and the series of post-Conquest boundary, wayside and churchyard crosses deriving their forms from the wheel-head. Many of these are known, when the heads are wanting, by their chamfered arrises. To illustrate them would carry us far beyond the pre-Norman series, and yet they are the descendants of the older type running through many curious transformations, and sometimes harking back to early forms in a way that deceives the unwary. It will be enough to show one striking instance of the conservatism of Northumbria in St Leonard's cross at Thrybergh in the Don valley (Fig. 227). Here is the reminiscence of the tenth century ring-twist, but rounded out in a British-work-

manlike 'finish'; a saint with his book under an arch, but the arch is a lancet; and the acanthus, never before seen in Northumbrian stone-carving, though it must have been familiar to anyone who saw books for a couple of centuries before this cross was set up.

It will have been remarked already that these survivals occur in out-of-the-way districts. They are absent at York and in the old centres. The devastation of the Conqueror (1079) accounts for that; it was more serious a blow to native art than even the Danish invasion. Until Norman lords began to build there was a sad hiatus, and then mere dregs of pre-Norman art and craft were available. But even in districts free from the ravaging a similar decline is visible. The fashion of making great gravestones had waned, and that was in the nature of things. It had started life as an exotic, in the sense that mason-craft and ornamental motives had been learnt from abroad, though we cannot say that the Anglian cross had been imported, so to say, ready-made, for in that case we ought to be able to answer the question 'Whence'? But once planted it took root and flourished. For a while it was a garden-flower, more and more widely cultivated. Then it was cross-fertilized, perhaps from Irish, certainly from Scandinavian sources, and it began to run wild through the country. From being a luxury-trade it became a folk-art. And then it ran itself out; the soil was tired, and without some new interposition nothing more could be expected in Northumbria.

FIGURE 227

But away from Northumbria and transplanted abroad there was still life in the seed. To follow the fortunes of the various new cultures which can be traced back to the original stock would make a long story, but we venture to add a few paragraphs rather for the reader's consideration than in the hope of his immediate conviction. Our

181

general proposition is this—that all monumental art and craft in the north-west of Europe sprang from Northumbria, though rude stones were undoubtedly antecedent, and in the course of its career the original design was greatly modified at various times and in different regions.

We have seen (page 137) that in the Isle of Man, among the earliest shaped and carved stones, there is a group of Anglian character, antedating the great outburst of wheel-crosses and wheel-cross slabs of the tenth century. Whether Gaut Bjarnarson and his contemporaries from 930 onwards owed anything to Northumbria except the bare suggestion of making a stone cross—which they did not learn from Denmark—we do not stay to consider: only pointing out that the peculiar cross-centre used by Gaut and his school is seen also in west Yorkshire at Kirkby Wharfe and Collingham (Figs. 107, 188, 189) on heads of which no other feature was in any way borrowed from Manx sources.

We have traced the work of the Master of Whithorn to Anglo-Cumbrian teaching in the middle of the tenth century; and from the Whithorn cross we have seen later local developments in south-west Scotland. Those of central southern Scotland come from Hoddam, itself one of the principal sources of the earliest Anglian cross-shaft; and as we follow the Clyde towards the sea we find one and another monument of later and later days bearing the mark of Northumbrian origin but gradually becoming transformed by Gaelic feeling into the beautiful twelfth century work of Keills and Iona, the picturesque Ardchattan design (the priory there was not founded before 1230) and the romantic crosses of Islay so fully described and finely illustrated by the late R. C. Graham, of Skipness. Here the Kildalton cross must be coeval with St Martin's at Iona, but the rest are mainly later; some very much later.

From Northumbria by the main ancient road through Redesdale the style travelled to Jedburgh, a late example of the finest Anglian work; and beyond, to many sites in the Lothians, where most of the crosses as far as Abercorn show the influence of the Anglo-Danish of the tenth century. And by the coast, at Coldingham and Aberlady and further still the influence of later Lindisfarne is plainly seen. A very great service has been done to this branch of the study by the contribution of Mr C. R. Peers (*Archaeologia*, vol. 74) in which the newly found Lindisfarne series is so thoroughly illustrated (Plates 51 to 61), showing design that holds by one hand to the Anglo-Danish group, with the plait and Jellinge animals, and by the other hand to the whole mass of eastern and central Scottish remains, with their still greater use of key-patterns and more complicated redundancy of repeated plaits. Notwithstanding the absorption of Pictish symbols and late-Celtic spirals into their design, the ultimate origin and consequent dating of these stones become clear to anyone who will compare them in Stuart's 'Sculptured Stones of Scotland' or Romilly Allen's 'Early Christian Monuments of Scotland' with the pictures given by Mr Peers. They are thoroughly Scottish, thoroughly Celtic, but would never have come into being without the lead of North-

umbria. The progress of their development can be traced steadily northwards, except that in the extreme north some monuments are obviously of Viking origin, and tenth century, like those of Northumbria.

Southwards we have seen the late Anglian survival taking root in the Midlands, first along the fringe of Northumbria in Derbyshire, Cheshire, Staffordshire and Nottingham. At a rather early period it reached Northamptonshire, already connected by old ties with the north; and on 'Hedda's Tomb' at Peterborough, and other monuments we see the late Anglian saints in their niches surviving along with Jellinge ornament of the tenth century.

In this direction the Anglian motives crept on still further and later; for example, to Barking on the Thames, where the fine elaborate plaits must be the work of the abbey as revived by king Eadgar about 970, and to Bexhill, where is a well-known and highly ornamented coped stone, not unlike similar work at Durham which must be dated to 1000 or later.

Towards the south-west of England we can follow the course of our Anglo-Danish style through Worcestershire to Gloucester by such salient examples as the head at Cropthorne near Evesham and the Gloucester stone itself, a fine example of the late Anglian beast treated in Jellinge style but not by Danish hands. Thence to the large and famous group of monuments centring in Wiltshire, where the same types are repeated with late Anglian scrolls and plaits at Ramsbury, the more elaborate quasi-Jellinge at Colerne and the simpler Northumbrian forms at Cricklade and Knook, or at Wantage and Sonning in Berkshire. We find the transition to Ringerike at Somerford (Wilts.) and Bibury (Oxon.) as Mr Reginald A. Smith pointed out long ago ('Proceedings Soc. Ant.' 1914, Jan. 22). But even these eleventh century pieces we have seen matched—discounting minor differences—by examples from the north, and it seems impossible to give them an origin unconnected with the source of all British ornamental stone-carving in Northumbria.

Coming to Cornwall we must walk warily. 'Celtic', no doubt, were the people among whom the early crosses were made; their inscriptions show their language. But turning over Mr A. G. Langdon's 'Old Cornish Crosses' and noting the preponderance of well-known plaits and scrolls, especially those of a distinctly decadent period; noting also heads sometimes of late Anglian form and sometimes with the Viking Age wheel—in many cases betraying a post-Conquest date by their cusped openings—it is impossible to disregard the evidences of late derivation from Northumbrian models. In another Celtic region, in Wales, we have already seen how the wheel-head was imported to Penmon and St Davids late in the tenth century, whether from Man or from other Norse settlements on the British coast, and how it ran through Pembrokeshire to Glamorgan. There the last developments before final decay are roughly datable to the late eleventh century by the headstone at St Davids to the sons of bishop Abraham, who was killed by Vikings in 1078.

With Anglian influence overseas we must deal even more lightly. Dr Bröndsted has traced the 'lion' on Harald Bluetooth's runic stone at Jellinge (about 980) to the 'great Anglian beast' (*op. cit.* 283, 288 f), adding 'The new style works as a strong ferment in Scandinavia...it can be observed on both great and small monuments from all the three kingdoms up through the eleventh century.' And as to the Ringerike style, current in Scandinavia in the early part of that century, it is not for us to venture into the discussion of its origin, whether native, Oriental or English. We have seen examples, as on the Leeds cross, which can only be supposed late and of Ringerike period by assuming that a loan from Scandinavia could be no otherwise. On their faces they bear the marks of the beginnings of the style and of a date before the style was general. And when one considers the stimulus to Scandinavian designers which was supplied by England in those stirring days, among many forms and models of art then of the past, taking also into account the close relations of the two shores of the North Sea, it may turn out hard to decide between rival claims.

Science and history, however, know nothing about 'claims'. They have to consider the examples, and all the examples. They have to conceive them in series and connexion. They have to remember the conditions of the stone-cutter's craft, the human circumstances which make it necessary to take that craft on its own terms, distinct from the traditions of the book-painter and the metal-worker. Otherwise there is no accounting for the taste or want of taste that hedged monumental art within such narrow lanes as we find it followed, while all the wealth of ornament in manuscripts and metal was open to any explorer who could have got his head above the fence.

THE INDEX

SITES of monuments are given in capitals, with the dates, herein proposed for the monuments mentioned, added in brackets; the Roman figure indicating the century, and *a*, *b* or *c* the early, middle or later part of the century.